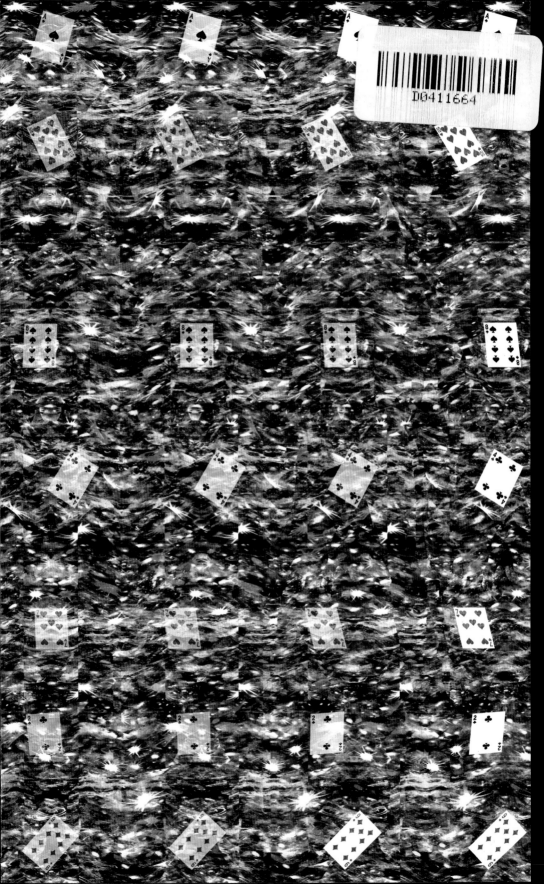

NOTHING IS
IMPOSSIBLE

NOTHING IS
IMPOSSIBLE

THE REAL-LIFE ADVENTURES OF
A STREET MAGICIAN

DYNAMO

EBURY
PRESS

1 3 5 7 9 10 8 6 4 2

This edition published 2012
First published in 2012 by Ebury Press, an imprint of Ebury Publishing
A Random House Group company

The Random House Group Limited Reg. No. 954009

Addresses for companies within the Random House Group can be found at
www.randomhouse.co.uk

A CIP catalogue record for this book is available from the British Library

The Random House Group Limited supports The Forest Stewardship Council
(FSC®), the leading international forest certification organisation. Our books
carrying the FSC label are printed on FSC® certified paper. FSC is the only
forest certification scheme endorsed by the leading environmental
organisations, including Greenpeace. Our paper procurement policy
can be found at www.randomhouse.co.uk/environment

Designed and set by seagulls.net

Printed and bound in Great Britain by Clays Ltd, St Ives PLC

Hardback ISBN 9780091948917
Trade paperback ISBN 9780091950453

To buy books by your favourite authors and register for offers visit
www.randomhouse.co.uk

Dedicated to the man who inspired all of the magic in this book,

Kenneth Walsh (1927 – 2012)

CONTENTS

PROLOGUE

THE IMPOSSIBLE DREAM

Standing on the banks of the River Thames, I shivered slightly in the early evening breeze. With the Houses of Parliament lit up in front of me, and the doleful toll of Big Ben ringing in my ears, I could feel my stomach churning nervously.

This was it. This was the moment I'd been building up to for what seemed like the whole of my life. It all felt so surreal.

Back home in Bradford, I knew the man who had got me here, Kenneth Walsh, my great-grandfather, or 'Gramps' as I call him, would watch this; maybe even the kids who used to pick on me and push me around. As I teetered on the edge of the riverbank, a crazy kaleidoscope of everything that had happened in the last twenty-eight years raced through my mind. As clichéd as it may sound, my whole life flashed before me.

I thought of all the people who had told me I'd never amount to anything; the tough times growing up on my estate; Gramps showing me magic for the first time; the teachers who sneered at my dreams of wanting to be a famous magician; the years working clubs around the country to make ends meet; shuffling my cards for hours in a hospital bed; impressing everyone from Prince Charles and Jay-Z to Will Smith and Chris Martin; the

knock-backs that at one time threatened to derail my career;
and the moment I was given the name Dynamo.

Since the age of twelve, magic had been my life. It was all
I'd thought about, all day, every day. Every waking hour
(and even in my dreams) I'd be conjuring up new ideas, new
illusions, new ways to bring something special to the world.
But never had I faced anything on the same scale as the
challenge that lay before me now. I was about to walk across
the River Thames.

Taking a deep breath, I nervously lifted my right leg. As my foot
touched the surface of the increasingly choppy water, I heard a
loud gasp. Above me, a crowd of people had gathered on the
banks of the river and on Westminster Bridge.

Shock, surprise and anticipation clouded their faces. I felt the
water flowing beneath my feet, soaking through my trainers,
sending shivers through my body. I could feel a strong wind
gusting across the river, making my heart beat even faster.

I was doing it. I was standing on water. There was no turning
back now.

As the audience swelled from ten to 2,000 people, I tried to clear
my mind. I had walked on water before at a swimming pool but
never on a natural body of unpredictable water. The Thames
is a different beast. It has incredibly strong, incalculable
undercurrents and there's always a lot of traffic. Completely
unpredictable. One wrong move and I could be sucked under
the murky water – the kind of vanishing act I would never want
to undertake. Over fifty people a year lose their lives to this
almighty river, so I had to carefully judge each step as the
waves rolled around me. Until now, I hadn't understood the
gravity of what I was attempting to do.

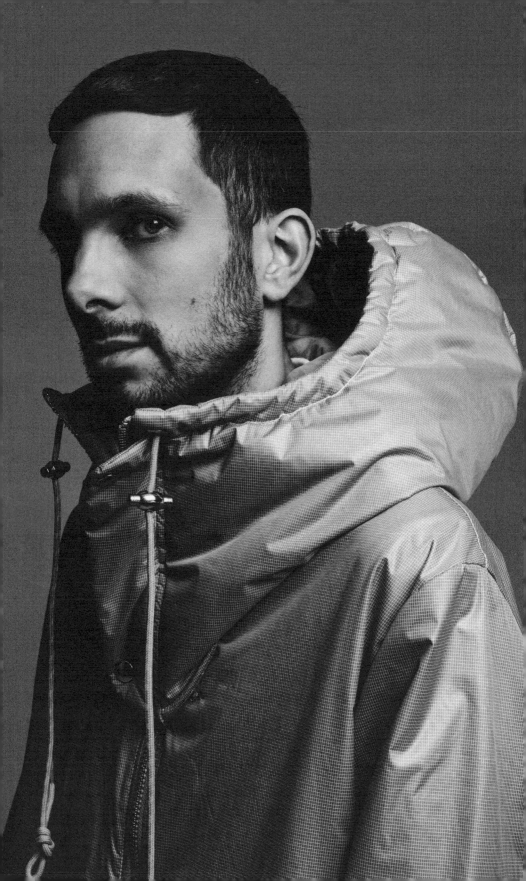

Nevertheless, I could feel the excitement running through the crowd as more and more people gathered. The energy made my hair stand on end. The power from the spectators was keeping me up there, keeping me afloat. I looked across to the Houses of Parliament, a view I had admired many times, but not really looked at until today. These grand old buildings had seen so much history unfold but would also be witness to me, Steven Frayne from Delph Hill, trying to make his own mark on the world.

For my very first television series, I wanted to do something iconic. It was vital that I captured the hearts of the nation. I had one shot to communicate and connect with people – fail, and I would be back in my hometown of Bradford, making ends meet with my street magic. Succeed, and I would take a giant leap towards being among the great entertainers of our time. I knew that if I was to make my name in the competitive field of magic, then I had to do something huge. Until relatively recently, the idea of walking on the moon was as inconceivable as walking on water. I wanted – needed – to prove that with hard work, determination and a little bit of magic, nothing was impossible.

I'd joked with my manager and close friend, Dan Albion, for years about walking across the Thames. I always said that if I ever got my own TV programme I would walk on water. And now, what seemed like the impossible had happened. I had my own show and I had to live up to my word.

I continued on. The water rippling under my soles. The crowd cheering. My knees knocking... Normally, when I'm nervous, I touch my tummy. But, given the importance of keeping my concentration at that particular moment in time, I managed to resist the urge. I swallowed my fear, steadied my nerves and carried on. Determination gripped every cell of my being and I took another step and another. And then I heard the roar of a speedboat engine and the flash of a blue light came into my peripheral vision...

It was my intention to walk the entire width of the Thames (a mere 826.8ft), but unfortunately the police had other ideas. I was in the zone at that point – adrenalin was coursing through my system and I was intently focused on reaching the other side of the river. So my memories are a blur of the actual moment I got picked up and dropped into the police boat. They put me on the floor and I could hear them asking me questions, but it wasn't computing. I was just so caught up in the moment that I had no idea what they were saying to me. 'What were you thinking? Are you all right?' they shouted, as they tried to figure out who I was and what I was doing. Luckily, there's no law against walking across the Thames and they let me go. I guess they'd never imagine a law was needed!

They took me back to the riverbank. I went home, texted my Gramps ('*I've just walked across the River Thames, it was amazing!*'), and then wrapped myself in warm towels and fell into a deep sleep.

It didn't hit me properly until a few days later and I started to see the coverage on the TV news and in the newspapers. On 25 June 2011, I like to think that, in some way, I created history. I'd done what I'd set out to achieve. I'd brought a feeling of wonder and amazement to the people. I'd proved the power magic has. For as long I can remember, all I have wanted to do is amaze people; to take away the stress of everyday life – if only for a minute – and show them something truly astonishing.

Ultimately I had showed that you really can do something that is seen as impossible by others – even if I had ruined a great pair of trainers in the process.

Walking across the River Thames was one of the scariest things I've ever done. But sometimes you've got to go for your dreams, no matter what the risk. It's better to try and to fail than it is to fail to try.

I've gone from being an insecure kid growing up on the Delph Hill estate in Bradford to travelling around the world, meeting people from all walks of life, sharing the most wondrous thing I know: the power of magic. Now, I want you to join me on the ride.

This book is about my life, sure, but it's also more than that. It's about how determination and hard work can change anyone's life. I hope it will provide inspiration and that the lessons I've learnt will help you on your life's journey. For this reason, I haven't written it in the usual chronological way – I've organised the chapters around places that have been important to me, and sometimes I will jump back and forward in time when a certain location brings back memories. I like to keep it playful, keep you guessing, and to shuffle things around like a deck of cards – just like I do in my magic. The world-renowned American magician and pickpocket Apollo Robbins once told me that the best magic isn't linear – it doesn't follow straight lines. I can only agree, and I have been influenced by this idea in the writing of these chapters.

This book really is about proving to you that nothing is impossible. It's about showing that whatever you want to achieve, you can make it happen. For me, magic has been my path – maybe it could be yours too? After all, everyone needs a little magic in their life...

CHAPTER 1

A MAGICAL
AWAKENING

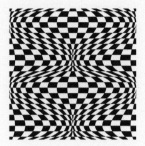

'Come on Steven, get in the bin,' the boy cackled as his brother lumbered towards me. For a second, I almost gave in. I'd been in that dustbin so many times it was almost my home away from home. The younger brother, let's call him 'Paul', and his older sibling, 'Ben', would pick me up, and as I struggled against their grip, they would force me inside. Thanks to my small frame, I was no match for the two of them. Then, once I was cowering inside the stinking plastic, they'd kick the bin and off I'd go, tumbling down what we called The Tits. They were two hills next to each other in the school grounds that were shaped like... well, you can probably guess. Inside, I'd feel every bump and pothole as I rattled around inside that bin, my pointy elbows banging into the sides, my ankles and knees twisting and turning. But the worst pain was the fear I felt deep inside me. My chest would constrict so tightly, I could barely breathe, but that feeling was something I slowly became used to. I was rolled down those hills so often I could have mapped out every rock and stone.

Being thrown down a hill in a rubbish bin wasn't a particularly pleasant experience. The bins always stank of old nappies and mouldy sandwiches and I would hear Paul and Ben's jeers as they ran behind it. Careering down the hill towards school, everyone would laugh as the bin picked up speed. A car or kerb would bring me to an abrupt halt. Dizzy and disorientated, I'd crawl out, ashamed and embarrassed, new bruises joining my old ones.

On that day, though, things were different. I didn't want to get in that stupid bin any more. I was fed up with being humiliated. As Paul towered over me, I made a decision. 'Pick me up then,' I said to him. Without questioning, he put his hands under my armpits and lifted me off the ground with ease, as always. 'Now put me down and I'll show you something. Go on,' I pleaded, 'I want to show you something amazing.' Reluctantly, he dropped me back on the pavement. 'OK. Try again,' I murmured, steadily fixing my eyes on his. This time, he couldn't move me. He tried and tried, grunting and sweating, but there was nothing he could do. He couldn't pick me up, no matter how hard he tried.

I had taken away all of his strength. 'How did you do that? Show us,' the brothers begged, exasperated. I just smiled, picked up my bag and walked down the hill to school.

I don't know where Paul and Ben are now. Last I heard, one of them was a nightclub bouncer and the other had apparently been murdered. Who knows? When you're from the kind of place I'm from, not much is expected of you. If you grew up on the Delph Hill estate, more often than not you ended up on the dole or inside. The only time people round my way got near royalty were when it was at Her Majesty's Pleasure.

Standing up to Paul and Ben that day would change my life forever. I might not have known it at the time, but over the coming years, millions of people would watch me perform the same magic as I had that day, aged twelve, when I finally beat the bullies...

I was born Steven Frayne, but nowadays most people call me Dynamo. I came into the world very quickly; my mum arrived at Bradford Royal Infirmary at 22.50 and I was born twenty minutes later, at 23.10 on 17 December 1982. I've been in a rush to get on with things ever since.

I was born six weeks premature, so I had to go straight into an incubator for twelve hours to get warmed up. I was super-tiny, just a couple of pounds, so they kept me in hospital for three weeks, until I weighed 4lb 15oz.

Because I was so small my mum had to feed me non-stop, every hour or so. When I was finally allowed out of hospital, she brought me home to the modest maisonette where I would live for the first five years of my life. The flat only had three rooms, and it was winter so it was absolutely freezing. Because I was so tiny and my mum was worried about me getting cold, she'd have the heating on full blast and would wrap me head to toe in a blanket, coat, scarf, hat and mittens. My granddad still jokes that that's the reason I'm so small – my mum shrunk me when I was a baby!

Money was tight when I was a kid. I was the oldest of four; my sister Jessica and my two little brothers Troy and Lee came along later. But they don't have the same dad as me. While it was just me and Mum she would always do whatever she could to make sure I felt loved and cared for. When I was four, she said I could have a birthday party. I was so excited. I invited all of my school friends from Hill Top, the local primary school that was a short walk from where we lived in the Laisterdyke council flats, on the Delph Hill estate. All Mum could afford for my birthday present was a six-pack of Kinder Eggs – but she had scrimped and saved to create a wonderful birthday spread for me: sandwiches, crisps, sweets and a birthday cake with four candles.

On the day, I waited and waited by the front door, running into the living room to look out of the window, craning to see the arrival of my friends. Minutes went by, then an hour, then two hours. No one came. Eventually, my mum gently told me that my friends weren't coming. A couple of the mums had rung with feeble excuses, but the truth was, they were too scared to come to the estate. I can't blame the parents for not wanting to bring their kids to our flat. Hill Top was a nice school with nice middle-class children. The thought of visiting Delph Hill, with its tower blocks and hooded teenagers, was probably pretty scary. I wasn't surprised to hear that the Laisterdyke flats were knocked down a few years ago. Even back in the eighties, they were rough and really run-down.

I was so disappointed I can still feel that lump in my throat now. I half-heartedly ate my Kinder Eggs, taking the toys to bed with me. I hated birthdays for years after that. Even now when I have a birthday or a launch party, I always worry that no one will turn up.

♠

It was around that time that my dad went into prison for the first time. He would remain inside, off and on, for the next fourteen years. He did time for loads of different things: petty crime, gang crime, drugs. He was a small-time criminal.

I remember very, very little about him because he was barely around for those first four years, and since he has come out of prison I've only seen him once. I don't even know his name. My mum and I rarely, if ever, speak about him.

My granddad tells me that when my parents first got together, my dad used to come round to my granddad's to see my mum. He'd arrive with loads of bikers – Bradford's equivalent of the

Hell's Angels. My granddad said they were nice enough, quite polite despite their leather jackets and long hair, but he'd never be able to get them out of the house. They'd stay there all night. My dad wasn't a biker, but I think he hung out with them because they protected him in some way. I don't know. I've no idea what the truth is. I hear lots of different stories from lots of different people. To me, he's become a myth. I don't know the truth about him, and I don't really want to know.

I had a lot of resentment towards him, particularly when I was a teenager. I know he was in jail and that he couldn't be around at certain times, but he could have sent me a birthday card or a Christmas present. No matter how small. On the few occasions he was out of jail for a month or two, I didn't see him because he'd be up to his old tricks. He very occasionally pops up now and then, but whenever he does try to come to find me, he asks for Dynamo, not Steven. I think that says a lot.

People say that I look a lot like my dad. I'm mixed race; my mum is white and my dad is Asian. That's as much as I know, because I've never met my dad's family and they haven't tried to get in touch since I was very young. They wanted to take me away for a few days not long after my dad first went to prison, but my mum said no because she was worried that they'd never bring me back.

Growing up in Bradford in the eighties and nineties was an interesting time. I was quite an anomaly in many ways. Most estates in Bradford are very racially divided; you have Asian people in one place and white people in another. Being mixed race and living on a largely white estate had its challenges.

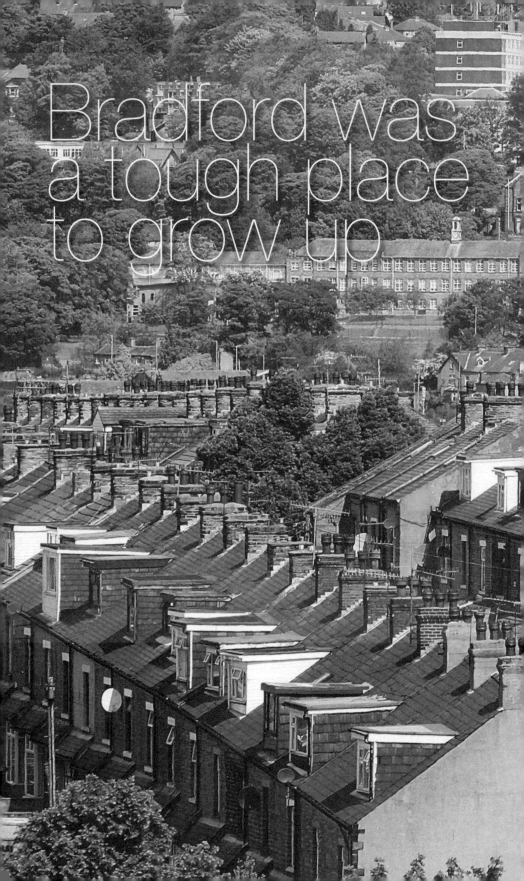

Bradford was
a tough place
to grow up

After my dad went into prison, we moved around different estates in Bradford, including Wyke, Wycoller and Markfield Avenue. Mostly, though, I spent my childhood and teenage years on an estate called Delph Hill. I grew up with my mum, her mum and stepdad (Nana Lynne and Granddad) and my mum's grandparents, my great-grandparents (Nan and Gramps). Apart from my aunty and some cousins, that was the only family I had.

Delph Hill is surrounded by countryside, so in theory, it could be a beautiful place. Back when I grew up, you didn't have to look too hard though to see the burnt-out cars, broken glass and dilapidated houses. It was your typical low-rise estate; lots of terraced houses crammed together on a hill. It was much neglected.

The estate is quite far from the city centre, so it's hard to go anywhere. It's a long bus ride to get to the train station and the buses come when they feel like it. Once you're in Delph Hill, you rarely ever leave. Growing up there left me feeling very isolated. I had the sense that real life was being lived far away from the patchy grass and streaky concrete that was my everyday view. It's been done up a lot since I was a kid. Nowadays, mostly older people live there, so it's much safer. They've cleaned it up considerably.

Back then, though, Delph Hill was a tough place to grow up. There were a lot of kids running around, selling drugs, taking drugs, robbing and fighting. With packs of young gangs roaming around, it wasn't safe to walk about – especially when you're a small kid with a young mum and no dad. It was safer to stay indoors because I was such an easy target. I was born small and I stayed small. Because of my size, I was picked on, both on the estate and at school. I'm hardly the biggest guy now, so you can imagine what I was like as a kid.

Even though I was tiny for my age, I had no idea that something was medically wrong with me. I played football like the other kids, I went skateboarding, and I ran around the playground – though that was mostly trying to escape from the bigger kids!

I was skinny and, no matter how much I ate, I found it hard to put on weight. Sometimes I would find blood in the toilet, but I thought all that was normal. My mum became concerned when I was thirteen. Until then, she assumed that I'd have a growth spurt when I hit puberty, but as my friends shot up around me, I stayed the same size.

My mum took me to the doctors and they started running a lot of tests – there were tubes up and down my body, cameras in and out of every place imaginable, and all types of horrible things. I had to have loads of barium meals, which are these rancid powdery drinks that help doctors see what's wrong inside of you. You can't eat anything the night before, so you can imagine how nice it is that the first thing you have to drink the next day is this disgusting, salty, acidic powder mixed with water. You have to do it, though – the barium is radiopaque, which means that whatever is wrong inside shows up clearly on an X-ray. After weeks of tests, the doctors eventually told me I had Crohn's Disease.

I'd never heard of Crohn's and I had no idea that it would mean a lifetime of discomfort, pain and, when it got really bad, lengthy hospital visits. Crohn's is a form of inflammatory bowel disease. It's classed as a chronic illness because it's very difficult to manage. The thing about Crohn's is that it's incurable. Each person has different symptoms, which makes it hard to treat, and therefore, I presume, cure. The exact cause is also unknown. It could be genetic, it could be the immune system or it could be affected by environment. It's more commonly found in Europe than, say, Africa.

Because it affects the stomach and digestive system, many sufferers of Crohn's tend to be very small, which explained my size. You can't eat certain foods and the food you can eat, you have trouble digesting.

As it is an inflammation in the digestive system, it means pretty much every time you eat, there are complications. Eating can sometimes be an uncomfortable experience. Imagine you've got a big, deep cut on your arm or your leg. Whenever you eat, it's like rubbing dirt into the wound.

Having Crohn's – so I've been told – can be similar to what women experience once a month; cramps, discomfort, blood loss and mood swings. Except it's what I have every day. I'm in pain all the time. I try to keep on top of it by not eating things that make it worse. There's a lot of stuff I can't eat, like sesame seeds, the skin of vegetables, peanuts, sweetcorn and beans. I can eat carrots though; they're good! Popcorn, on the other hand, is not my friend. That put me in hospital for two weeks a couple of years ago. Sometimes I don't know if certain things are going to make me ill. So I could plan to do lots of things the next day, but I actually can't because I'll end up ill in bed.

I'm in a relationship now, but it used to be awkward taking girls out. I'd usually take them for some food and I'd be eating and suddenly realise I needed the toilet. The worst time to go the toilet is when you're on a date with someone you don't know very well. Leaving her waiting for half an hour isn't the greatest look.

My condition also means I've also got weak bones. I'm anaemic which makes my teeth and bones brittle and my body aches a lot. It makes my eyes water sometimes. My back kills all the time. I'm often very tired and I find it hard to sleep. I can't lie on my stomach because I have an operations scar there and I find it hard to sleep on my back, so I have to really tire myself out before I can fall asleep. I wake up every morning in pain and I have to sit in a hot bath to try to loosen up my body. As a kid I found living with Crohn's difficult. Not just because of the physical symptoms, but because it was another thing that made me an outsider. I was different. It made me small and I couldn't run as fast as the other kids – easy prey for the bullies. But as I've grown older, I've learnt how to manage it better, and more importantly I don't dwell on it. I'll never let it stop me doing anything I want to do.

Medication used to help, but the ones that worked best also had the worst side effects. And the side effects weren't worth it. I felt so drugged up when I was on them that I didn't feel like me. For that reason, I don't really drink alcohol and I've never done drugs. I don't like not feeling myself.

Of course, I wasn't the only kid on our estate with problems. I wasn't the only one trying to control something uncontrollable. Life throws a lot of weird stuff at you – some good, some bad, but as I've grown older I've realised you just have to find a way to carry on and do what you want to do. No matter what it takes. And, after being diagnosed with Crohn's, it wasn't long until I found my own secret to getting through those dark times.

♠

I went to Wyke Middle School and Wyke Manor Upper School, which I suppose were your average comprehensive schools in the nineties. Culturally, there was a rich mix of Indian, white, Jewish, South-East Asian and black students. The school, like all comprehensives, was mixed ability, so you had all types of kids there. It wasn't particularly huge – maybe 500 pupils – but it was pretty rough. Some kids would show up to lessons, some wouldn't. There would be a lot of smoking, and some kids used to bring in booze, others something stronger. Bullying was rife. It was the sort of place where you had to look after yourself. You would never have gone to the teacher to tell them someone was picking on you.

Initially I learnt, as a defence mechanism, that if I was willing to laugh at my own expense, then other people would laugh too. It was degrading, but I was just trying to fit in, trying to make friends by being what I thought was 'cool'. It was only years later that I realised people were humouring me and taking the mickey out of me most of the time. They weren't laughing with me, they were laughing at me. Guys like Paul and Ben would pretend to be my friends, but then they'd demand my dinner money. No dinner money, into the dustbin I went. So, to try to get out of trouble, I talked too much and I talked a lot of rubbish. Little Steven thought he was very cool but, looking back now, I probably wasn't as cool as I liked to think.

The teachers didn't help much either; they didn't seem to understand. 'Shut up and sit down, Steven,' they'd say. 'Keep on like that and you're straight for detention.' Some teachers don't know how to communicate with kids and then you totally lose their attention. In my opinion kids would take someone who they relate to, like a music artist much more seriously in the classroom than your average, out-of-touch teacher.

I wasn't brain of Britain, but I was perhaps quicker to grasp what was being taught than the other kids. It looked like I was acting out, but really my mind wasn't being challenged enough. I knew I could do the work quickly so I'd doss about, distracting the other kids and driving the teachers mad in the process.

I tried being the class joker, I tried being top of the class, I tried being friends with the bullies, but nothing I did helped me to fit in. I was an awkward little boy; trapped between the gaps of all these different worlds.

♠

'**S**teve, are you coming to the dam with us?' shouted Paul. I was sat outside my mum's house, trying to mend my broken skateboard. 'Yeah, yeah, wait for me,' I said excitedly, chucking aside my skateboard and running after them.

Next to Delph Hill was another estate called Woodside, the two separated by a dam. Once a year, kids from the two estates would meet to have a fight. It was like something out of *The Warriors* or *West Side Story* – albeit the Bradford version. All the local estate kids would pile in and try to beat each other up. You know that scene in *Bridget Jones's Diary* when Colin Firth and Hugh Grant have that pathetic slapping fight? Well, it was sort of like that. Usually, one side would get cold feet and run away and the other estate would be crowned the 'winner'.

Ordinarily, though, the dam was where the older kids from Delph Hill went to smoke, muck about and try to get off with girls. Being asked to go down there with them was a big deal. Like anyone, I was desperate to fit in and be one of the cool kids. At that point, I was, or so I thought, friends with Paul and Ben.

We got to the dam and within two minutes of us being there, Paul and his brother had picked me up. I knew what was coming; it had happened before.

The dam water was cold, murky and filthy dirty. As I flailed around, panic rising as I struggled for air, two hands gripped my shoulders and pulled me out. Coughing and choking, Ben threw me down on the muddy bank. All I could hear were the other kids laughing like it was the funniest thing they'd ever seen. I pretended not to care and tried to smile, relieved that they wouldn't see the tears on my already wet face. 'It's only a joke, Steve, don't be a baby,' they'd say. It wasn't very funny to me. I couldn't swim. Every time they did it, I was convinced I would die.

The bullying started a lot earlier than I even realised at the time. It would be more psychological than physical; my 'friends' would say or do something to make me look stupid – they'd take the mick out of me and I'd laugh along. Because it was done under the guise of a joke – mates mucking about, everyone having a laugh – I couldn't see what was happening. But Paul and Ben were never thrown in the water. No one ever took their lunch money off them.

Even when the bullying became more physical, I just thought it was normal. If it wasn't me being chucked in the dam, then it was someone else. I wouldn't stop and help the other kid being bullied; I'd just be relieved it wasn't me on that occasion. I thought it was normal because it happened to loads of kids all the time. But Paul and Ben weren't my friends. They hadn't asked me to go down there to hang out. They got me down there to chuck me in, make fun of me, to use me as a scapegoat.

It's only when writing this book, that I realised my desire to walk on water came from that time. I always thought the River Thames was an idea that had randomly popped into my head, but I know now that as a little kid, soaking wet, freezing cold and scared stupid, I would have given anything to walk on water. To be able to just glide across the surface and get away from them all. The seed was sown.

♠

Because of the fear of being bullied, I started to avoid going out at all and spent more and more time alone in my room. The likes of Paul and Ben couldn't get me there. Up in my room, I'd watch as many films as I could. I became enveloped in a fantasy world of action heroes and futuristic metropolises. I really wanted to be MacGyver, the private detective, from the American TV show of the same name. It was huge in the eighties. To me, MacGyver was the ultimate action star. No matter what situation he was in, he always found a way out. He created something from nothing. Just like a magician, in a way. He would take down a plane with just a hastily assembled slingshot, using a belt and an inflatable dinghy. That ideology stuck with me as I got older. Now, you can take me to a slum in Rio and I'll pick up an old bit of wire and think of something to do. Take me to Miami and I'll make a girl's tan line move from her wrist to her shoulder. Show me snow and I'll turn it into diamonds. MacGyver instilled in me a sense of improvisation; you don't need expensive props to make brilliant magic. Back then, though, what MacGyver did for me was make me realise that you didn't just have to accept things the way there are. You can makes things happen out of thin air.

MacGyver wasn't my only screen hero. I was very naïve as a kid and, as ridiculous as it sounds, I believed that Superman was real. I thought Gotham City really existed. I'd have trouble sleeping, partly because of the Crohn's, so I'd be up half the night watching *Superman*, *Batman*, *Back to the Future*, Indiana Jones and *The Goonies*, over and over again. It was an escape into a mysterious world where normal people could have magical powers. I'd imagine what it would be like to be them; to be able to travel through time like Marty McFly and fly through the air faster than the speed of light like Superman. In my mind, these people were real, so what they could do was a reality too. Even now I believe I can make those things happen. Who knows one day maybe I will move the moon like Superman did. In all of my work, you'll see the positive impression those films left on me – it was watching Keanu Reeves in *The Matrix* and Spider-Man's skyscraper scaling that inspired me to perform levitations and walk down the *Los Angeles Times* Building. But there are no tricks with my magic!

As a kid, though, I had no idea what bearing these superheroes would have on my life. All I knew was that they could make me happy and transport me out of my own little world of worry, but now their value to me is incomparable. Those films taught me to never doubt your abilities. If you want to make something happen badly enough, then you'll make it happen. I still watch films to inspire me now. It's an art that knows no boundaries, just like magic.

I was nine when magic really became an intrinsic part of my life. Like lots of little kids, I had a passing interest when I was very young. I was given one of those generic magic sets for Christmas and I'd mess about with the wands and cards, but it wasn't something I paid much attention to.

But then one day Gramps gave me my first real glimpse of magic in real life. He'd fought in the Second World War and had learnt a few things then that he used to entertain his army mates with. And, after the war, he was a pool hustler and could often be found in the local pub, taking people for their cash with one of his tricks. I'll never forget when he first performed one of his classic moves on me. He took two different-sized shoelaces, then did some crazy move with his hands, and all of a sudden...the laces were exactly the same length. As he waved them in front of my face, my mind whirred. It was the most amazing thing I'd seen – real magic in my own front room.

'Show me how to do that, Gramps,' I begged, excitedly. He looked at me for a minute and then gave me a smile. 'I'm not going to tell you how to do it, but I'll show you something else.' I didn't need to be told twice when he sent me off to the kitchen for two boxes of matches.

What was Gramps going to show me next? When I returned, Gramps painted the tips of the matches and the boxes – one set green and the other set red. Then, he put the green matches in the red box and vice versa and asked me to hold them. 'Shake them up,' he said and I did, as hard as my little hands would allow me. The matches rattled away inside, while my heart pounded with anticipation.

'Now open them,' Gramps beamed, his eyes wide. Tentatively, I push the little boxes open and when I did I nearly dropped them. My breath caught as I looked down at them. Somehow the green matches were in the green box and red matches in the red box. I was absolutely stunned. Miraculously, the matches had invisibly travelled through the air, without me seeing, and had switched boxes. I was blown away. Just like all good magicians, Gramps never gave me an explanation. It was simply magic. Of course, I can make that happen myself now. But that day it was like I'd fallen under a spell. Over the next couple of years, my interest in magic grew, and then when I turned twelve it really took hold of me.

Gramps's army days meant he had seen a lot of life. He was a wise man. I never told him that I was being bullied, he just knew. He'd meet me after school sometimes and I reckon he saw things happening for a long time, but wanted to make sure before he stepped in. He was like Mr Miyagi – and I was his Grasshopper!

One night, not long after my twelfth birthday, Gramps showed me the ultimate way to take on the bullies. I'd been rolled down the hill for the hundredth time, and my head was hanging so far down it almost touched my toes as I shuffled home. I'd been crying – not because the boys had hurt me but because I felt so humiliated. Nana and Gramps were at our house and I went straight to my room, as always. When my mum called me down for tea, I sat there, quietly, eating. I didn't say anything to Gramps, but he could just tell. After tea, he came up to my room. 'You know how to win a fight, don't you, Steven?' he said. I looked up hesitantly, shaking my head very slightly. 'All right, come here and I'll show you something.'

Gramps didn't give me a master class in boxing. He did something much better than that. This time, rather than showing me magic with laces and matchboxes, he demonstrated how to, literally, take away someone's strength. By the end of my 'lesson' Gramps was unable to pick me up – his slight, twelve-year-old grandson. It was the most empowering feeling I've ever had. I still use the technique today – on the first series of *Dynamo: Magician Impossible*, I asked world champion heavyweight boxer David Haye to pick me up and after I'd taken his strength away not even he could do it. I'm eight stone max at my heaviest! He looked very confused.

A couple of days later, I saw Paul and Ben and *the* life-changing moment I described earlier took place. I drained them of their strength. It was the last time they ever rolled me down a hill or threw me into the dam. The look on their faces was an absolute picture. Their jaws dropped and they backed away nervously. I'd found the most powerful way to overcome them – through the power of my mind.

Not long after, I recalled the magic Gramps had shown me with the matchboxes. I'd worked it out by myself and shown it to my mum and my cousins, but not to anyone at school. I reached a stage where I could practically do it with my eyes shut, but hadn't found my moment. Then one day, I saw my chance. 'Hey everyone, watch this,' I said to the kids as they milled around their desks, waiting for the teacher to arrive. By now, word had got round about what I'd done to Paul and Ben. My classmates thought I was a bit weird, and that I had some kind of strange power, so they had steered clear of me ever since. Eventually, though, curiosity getting the better of them, they slowly gathered round. 'It's probably a load of rubbish,' muttered one. I traced Gramps's move and showed everyone how the green matches were in the red box and the red matches were in the red box, then I closed them and asked one of the kids to shake them. Then – *pow* – in a flash the matches had swapped over...

'Wow!' exclaimed one girl who I'd had a crush on for ages. 'Show us again.' The rest of them all stood open-mouthed; some were laughing, some shouting in amazement or shaking their heads. I don't know what the best bit was: the acceptance of my classmates or the realisation that girls who had previously ignored me began to pay me some attention. It seemed the magic gave me the edge I'd been craving. As I drank in the scene, it was almost as magical as the matchboxes – around me stood boys and girls of all different colours and backgrounds. Usually, the Asian kids kept to themselves while the white kids always stuck together and black kids would drift between the two groups. It was the same when we were all back home on the estate too. But in this moment, magic seemed to have broken down the divide. Slowly, my eyes were opening – magic had powers far beyond those you could see.

From that moment, I immersed myself in magic. I read every book I could get my hands on and practised and practised, day after day and night after night. Magic literally became my world... some might say an obsession. I sat in and practised magic for hours on end with Gramps helping me and encouraging me along the way. I'd spend hours just shuffling cards alone, trying to figure out new ways of moving them around. Hours turned into months, months into years. I was told recently about Malcolm Gladwell's 10,000 hours theory – that all experts have practised for at least 10,000 hours to master their chosen field, be that Beethoven, Michael Jackson, Picasso or Steve Jobs. I laughed when I heard that; I reckon I've spent at least ten times that practising my magic.

♠

I was a loner growing up, but over the years I've met thousands of people from all walks of life. It might have scared the kids at school, but as I got older and went to college, my magic instantly won me friends. I chose to go to the Batley School of Art and Design in Bradford, which wasn't the typical college that you went to if you had gone to my school. Not only was it a creative college, but you had to take two buses to get there from where I lived. But I didn't care about the journey. It was a fresh start for me; no one knew who I was and no one knew I had been bullied before. The first day I got there, someone asked me what I was into, and I said, 'I like doing magic.' I did some, and they loved it and they accepted me. I felt like I could be myself. When I told them about my Crohn's they just said, 'Oh, that sucks,' and that was that. They didn't act like I was some alien out of space. They were much more mature about it. I found that people wanted to hang round with me, watch me perform with my cards. It created an immediate connection. Magic was my way of bringing people together.

That first time when I took away Paul and Ben's strength, thanks to Gramps, my whole life changed and I knew my life's focus would be magic. It wasn't the idea of fame or money attracting me back then – far from it. It was simply that the most wonderful feeling rose up inside me whenever I showed someone magic; it made people happy. I'll never, ever get bored of watching people's faces when they witness something astonishing.

I'd spend hours shuffling, figuring out new ways of moving the cards

CHAPTER 2

HUSTLE AND BUSTLE

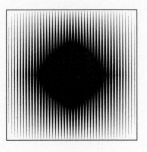

'I've worked it out; I know how you do it!'

Every now and then my friends or my girlfriend will suddenly, out of nowhere, announce that they've figured out how I do a certain piece of magic. The funny thing is it's always something random. I haven't done magic like my shoelaces tying themselves since 2004. But just recently, one of my oldest mates came up and said, 'I've worked it out!' The thought of people sitting around talking about how I walked on water blows my mind.

There are so many elements involved in every single thing I do. The average person doesn't understand all of the technical intricacies that go into one piece of magic. They might see how one element is done and the illusion is broken for them. They think because they've seen one little thing they know everything,

'I saw you do something behind your back.'

'Oh, right. What did you see?'

'Well, I don't know, but you did something, so that's how you did it!'

Unless you're into magic then it can be hard to appreciate the way someone actually does something, rather than just the end effect. It often takes someone who's really into the art to understand it. I watch other magicians all the time because I appreciate the spectacle, the art, the style of that magician. It's beautiful to watch magic when it's perfectly executed.

Take music, for instance. You've got so many unknown kids out there who have the same potential as some of the biggest, most famous rappers. But the normal person on the street wouldn't appreciate the fine detail that they put into their wordplay. It would take the ear of an emcee to hear a rapper from the UK and say, 'Wow, that kid's cadence, his punch lines, the way he structured the lyric, his use of double entendres is amazing.' Sometimes it takes an artist to fully appreciate an artist.

I don't mind that people want to work it out. But I hope that my magic is strong enough that ultimately people just enjoy it. I really want people to believe in my magic because then anything is possible. There's something that Joseph Dunninger, a pioneer of magic, once said: 'For those who believe, no explanation is necessary; for those who do not, none will suffice.'

That's very, very true. I think magic is a feeling, it's an emotion. It's something that is brought out in someone when they're witnessing something they can't explain. They think, *I can't explain that, it must be magic.*

♠

I think that part of my success as a magician comes down to a combination of factors that informed my childhood years. I was ill a lot of the time and I lived on a rough estate, so my mum didn't like me playing outside. I spent a lot of time indoors cooped up in my bedroom. I had days, weeks, months and, ultimately, years to perfect my magic.

As a kid, I would practice with my cards, with bits of string, or matchboxes, for hours and hours after school. I bought those 'starter' magician boxes but would bore of them immediately and instead use the props that they came with to further my own ideas. I was absorbed in the world of magic and what I could do with it.

My room was pretty small. There was a window to the right of the bed that I'd sometimes stare out of absent-mindedly while shuffling cards. I'm a Bradford City fan so I painted my walls in claret and amber in honour of my football team. It was me, on my bed, watching films and working on my magic.

As I got older, my mum let me go out a little more after school, even suggesting I could get a part-time or Saturday job. She didn't have money to spare, so if I wanted to buy myself clothes or CDs, then I'd have to earn my own way.

I had a couple of different jobs as a teenager. I got myself a paper round and then, when I was fourteen, I got a job in a local video store, which I really loved.

Although it wasn't that glamorous, the video store inadvertently informed a huge part of my approach to magic. I'd get to see all the new films before anyone else. I'd go home with two or three of the latest releases and watch them until my eyes were too heavy and I'd fall asleep. I'd spend hours absorbed in the world of Superman, Spider-Man and Batman. I became even more obsessed with film than when I was a kid and almost without realising it I built up an encyclopaedic knowledge.

Someone else who worked in a video store is the film director Quentin Tarantino. It's perhaps no coincidence that we both

ended up in the creative industries; although Tarantino's a film-maker and I'm a magician, I don't see what we do as particularly different. We both entertain people in a very visual sense. Film and magic are able to transport people away from life as we know it, to the realms of the impossible.

When I was seventeen I started working at a hardware store as pretty much the dogsbody. When I wasn't lifting and carrying I'd be sent out back to bag up nails. I'd have to count them one by one and I'd be covered in cuts and dust. It was hard work but the boss was really cool. He even bought me a magic book!

♠

Over the years, I've tried to push the envelope with what I do, but there's nothing purer than having a pack of cards in my hand and just jamming. I can entertain myself for hours. I can create art with cards. I can generate moments of astonishment. All I need is me and a pack of cards, and I'm pretty sure I could walk into any room anywhere in the world and do stuff that no one's ever seen before. I practise with my cards the whole time. I'll be watching TV and not realise that I'm doing it. My cards have become an extension of me.

A deck of cards is a pretty magical thing in itself. The more I found out about their history, the more fascinated I was by them. Did you know they were invented in ancient China during the Tang dynasty? They spread throughout Asia in the 1300s and came into Europe, via Egypt, in the fourteenth century. There are four suits in each deck and there are four seasons in the year. If you add up all the pips (that's the suit symbols) on all the cards, they add up to 364, plus one for the Joker, that comes to 365. There are 365 days in a year. Everything stands for something.

When I was a teenager, I used to go to the MAPA Youth Club in West Bowling. You could play football or learn breakdancing. I was really into my magic and I was beginning to want to take it in my own direction. I would practise breakdancing every week and then I'd do my magic after the classes or during the breaks.

There were three guys who used to teach us breakdancing – Rash, Jimmy and Dennis John, who choreographs a lot of my shows now. Rash and Jimmy were two Asian guys who were amazing body poppers. One day, I had been learning how to do the glide where you move from one foot to the other in a seamless way. I'd practise it in between some body popping. Messing about, I did the glide and, at the end, combined it with popping. Jimmy said, 'Oh that's amazing, you should keep practising that'. It suddenly fell into place and made sense. I could combine elements of dance with shuffling.

It's like when you're cooking at home and you accidentally put the wrong ingredient into something, but then it tastes better and you've suddenly created this great new chicken sauce. I combined two things that shouldn't have been together, but they worked – they tasted good!

I soon discovered that body popping could transform my act. Anyone can shuffle cards with a bit of practice, and I quickly learnt how to do it like a professional gambler. I would 'riffle' the cards, which is when you split the deck in two and then interweave them as they fall. I could do the cascade where you lay the whole deck out flat in one smooth motion, and I learnt how to work the deck so it would fly through the air from one hand to the other.

When I did those moves at school, the kids were impressed at first, but they soon lost interest. But when I showed them my new ideas, they were in awe all over again. Thanks to breakdancing and body popping, I learnt how to incorporate the moves into my card shuffle, giving me another way to appeal to kids my own age. A few years ago, I taught myself to shuffle in slow motion. Now it's second nature to me, but it took a lot of attempts to be able to stack them at odd angles or flick a card up on the air and kick it behind me.

Really, I am my own audience so it made sense for me to work alongside the culture that inspired both me and the kids around me. I always wanted to make sure that no matter what people thought of my magic, there should be enough skill displayed that they have to respect it regardless. Even if they think what I'm doing is a 'trick', hopefully they'd still appreciate the dexterity of my hands, the expertise behind it, and my approach.

♠

You've got to put your heart and soul into it if you want to succeed at this game; you won't make money overnight and you have to look at the bigger picture if you're heading for the top. I've achieved a lot so far, but I haven't touched where I want to go. It's not easy – you will get knock-backs – but you have to take the criticism. You have to have good people around you. Listen to everyone's advice and take it in, although you don't always have to do what they say. But listening and making a considered judgement on what you hear is so important. I don't take criticism as a personal attack. I know when someone's intentions are honest and when they're just being jealous. Even if it's delivered in a horrible way, I think it's still important to think through what someone has said rather than dismiss it straight away as someone 'hating'.

When you're doing what you do – whatever it is – you've got to set high expectations because these days everyone is competing on a world scale. If you want to make it as a singer you've got to think that you're going up against Adele, Lady Gaga and Justin Bieber. If sport is your thing, consider the Beckhams, the Bolts and the Messis. I looked to Blaine, Copperfield and Penn and Teller in the hope that one day I might be mentioned in the same breath as them. If you read up on these kinds of people then you will find the beginnings of their stories are somewhat similar to mine. In all those cases, those guys, like me, worked relentlessly on their chosen craft from a really young age. If you're fortunate to discover that you're not only good at cooking, piano or table tennis, but you love it, then keep at it and work as hard as you can. In later years it will pay off, even if it's not in the way you might have expected. And it's never too late!

It takes hours and hours of work. I'm talking in the thousands. I was stubborn, I kept on going, and I worked harder at magic than anyone could have done. If you really want to do something, don't let anyone tell you that you can't. So many people told me I couldn't do it and they were wrong. You have to be stubborn but be smart with it. If you think you can prove others wrong, go for it.

For a long time I felt quite shunned by some circles of magic. At first they thought I was destroying their idea of magic; that it wasn't supposed to be done on the street by a guy in a hat and a hoodie. I'm more accepted now, as I'm inspiring the younger generation to get into magic, which is good for the whole art form.

♠

People began taking me more seriously as a magician when I hit my mid-teens. I started to get asked to work around the estate at birthday parties, or my mum's friends would want me to come over and perform at a party or a christening. Word spread slowly around Delph Hill, then Bradford, then Sheffield, and before I knew it, I was performing all over the North of England at clubs and parties.

Initially, people would just offer to pay for my petrol; so if I was playing a show in Leeds, I wouldn't make much money. But me and my boys found a great system to make a few tips. I always liked people to tip because they wanted to. That said, sometimes of course you have to give people a little nudge.

Though I didn't have many friends at school, I made lifelong friends when I was a teenager. Alex, Johnny and Marcus were my boys back then and still are today. I had all of them involved in my work: Alex would drive us, Marcus would be security, and Johnny would collect the cash and deal with the bookings.

With the help of my friends, I formulated a routine that enabled me to make tips without really asking for them. I'd have a card, which just said 'Dynamo' and my logo on the front. I'd also have a glass full of props like pens, coins and cards, which I'd use for my magic. At the end of my act I'd say something like, 'Here's your card, the ace of spades. I'm Dynamo, thank you very much'... I'd then flip my logo card over and on the back it said 'Tips please'.

My boy Marcus would pick up the empty prop glass, and Johnny, who's in there pretending he's not with us, would rush over and throw a fiver in it. Before you know it, everyone else would start chucking in cash.

It was all about the turnover. I'd do ten minutes and hit them with the tips. Usually, by that point I would have created a crowd of at least fifty people. They wouldn't all tip but it was nice to have a few quid in your pocket.

I started doing this at sixteen years old, sneaking into student gigs and the odd club night. As my name continued to grow, I went from earning just a bit of petrol money, to getting paid to turn up, plus petrol money, plus tips. Student nights especially were always great, because they were always up for a bit of fun and would part with what they could.

Because people wanted the 'product' I was delivering, I started looking at merchandising and branding – albeit in a very informal, low-budget way. I would burn CD-ROMs with five Windows Media clips of me doing magic and sell them for a pound after each performance. I'd also sell Dynamo stickers

which people would collect and cover themselves in from head to toe. We killed it.

We'd make a lot of money playing in Leeds, Bradford, Sheffield or Manchester and then drive home.

We'd get back to Nan's, where I was living at the time, at three in the morning, or whenever the club shut. 'Shush, Marcus, you'll wake me Nan up,' I'd whisper as we sat around Nan's dinner table and shared all the tips. 'One pound for Alex, one pound for Johnny, one pound for Marcus and two pound for me.' Everyone agreed that was a fair way to divvy up the cash.

Whatever time we got home Nan would appear. 'Oh, you're back, boys. Who wants some bacon sandwiches?' she'd ask. I think she worried about me and couldn't sleep until I was home and safe. Nan did everything for me and tried to keep my feet on the ground. If I said I wanted to be a magician she'd say, 'Yeah and I've heard ducks farting in deep water before.'

Nan fed me, she did my washing, and she paid the rent. I can't even tell you what I spent all that money on. Stupid stuff that I couldn't afford growing up: adidas trainers, Eckõ hoodies and New Era caps, rather than the non-branded cheap clothes from Woolies or hand-me-downs that I'd had as a child. 'I'm gonna buy us all an Xbox each, then we can all play at the same time,' I told the boys. We couldn't have all just played on one together, of course. Stupid.

These were the days, though, before I had any formal business plan. In my mind, I loved magic and performing, and it happened to be a great way of making money to buy nice trainers, but I didn't even consider I could make a career out of it. We were just living day-to-day on whatever money we had. It was just pocket money really but it was nice to feel like I was making my own way in the world.

With every booking I did, I quoted a low fee, so I was pretty much guaranteed to get three bookings off the back of it. I'd always set myself up for the next week on the night of the first gig. I wouldn't charge people the earth so they'd book me, but then they'd tip me on top, and their friends would tip me, and before you know it you've covered your costs with a little extra. Occasionally, you would see the high rollers who want to show off to their friends. 'Here you are mate, here's fifty quid, good on ya,' they'd say. But that rarely happened.

It's funny but it felt like I had a lot more spending money, doing things the way I was back then, than I do now. I'm very comfortable financially now, of course, but because I had no outgoings the little bit of money I had went a long way.

Everywhere I went, my boys came with me. I wasn't the leader of the group, but I was like the boss: a leader makes sure everyone knows to follow, but a boss makes sure everyone eats.

I suppose I had a certain sort of fame back then. *'I'm the king of Bradford, man!'* said the arrogant voice inside my head. In reality, I was nothing; I was a local kid with a bit of local fame. But I was popular for the first time in my life, and that was an incredible feeling. I'd finished school, so all the people who'd had opinions about me and who had judged me didn't matter anymore. The ones who were important were my friends and they stuck with me.

It was one of the most exciting times in my career. It was certainly when I was the most hungry. I'd get in at five in the morning and start preparing new ideas.

It was before I'd been tainted by any of the negatives that success can bring, and before I'd had many knock-backs. I felt like I was totally in control. I was, if I'm being honest, probably caught up in the idea of potentially being able to make money from my magic. As I got older, I realised that money can only buy you things that make you happy in the short term, but there's a bigger picture too.

It wasn't only at school and as a teenager that magic helped me. I'm not the biggest guy, so magic saved me at times. It got me out of scuffles, it's distracted someone who was about to rob me. Magic would get me into a club even though the bouncers thought I wasn't dressed right. It's got me out of where I grew up in Delph Hill and taken me all the way around the world.

I let people come to me and with that, the money followed. If it had been the reverse and I was trying to win people's attention because I wanted money, it would never have worked.

I've always been a sharp dresser. Aged four.

Aged one and a half and excited about my christening.

Gramps and me hanging out in America.

Patrolling the mean beaches of Virginia.

Proud big brother. Me, Troy and Lee.

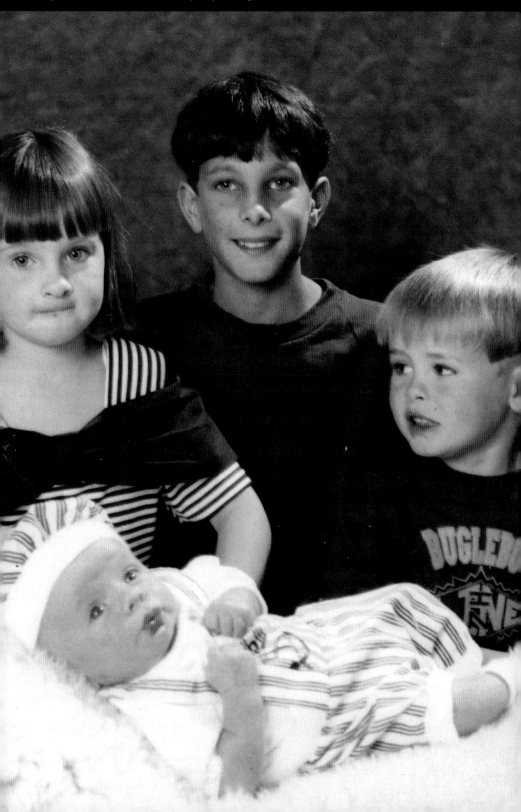

At home in Bradford with Troy, Gramps and Nan.

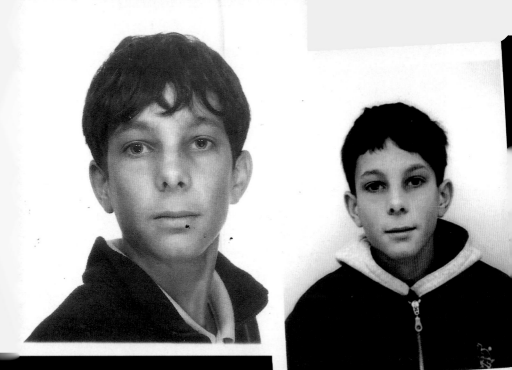

Old passport pics. Don't laugh!

Mum and me with Bear Gass.

I made my name by working the clubs and party circuits.

Turning lottery tickets into cash for Prince Charles and Kevin Spacey at Clarence House.

better to
try and to
fail than
to fail to try

It wasn't really that much of a conscious decision on my part; these are things I learnt along the way or have only come to realise now that I reflect on them. My initial hunger came from wanting to feel important and cool and popular, because I was bullied. I wasn't the cool kid, I wasn't popular, I didn't have a dad and I guess I was a bit of a geek.

But it was being a geek that drove me to hone my skills almost to the point of obsession. That obsession has made me the magician that I am today. When I started to succeed, that's when I began to find myself. People started to like me, and like my magic.

Despite the excitement of making money for the first time, it wasn't my main motivation. Neither was it simply about chasing fame. It was about acceptance. That was where my hunger really came from. One of the most important things I've taken away from making my TV show *Dynamo: Magician Impossible* is that people not only respected my work, but also they accepted *me*. I didn't pretend to be anything I wasn't; I took the camera to my old estate, I featured my boys, I talked about being bullied. And people still accepted me. This was really the first time I not only felt that way, but, as cheesy as it sounds, I accepted myself. I let go of trying to be cool, I let go of hoping people would like me.

I approached *Dynamo: Magician Impossible* in exactly the same way as I have always approached my magic; I wanted people to accept me for who I was, and they have. Magic, like so many things in my life, was the key to that.

CHAPTER 3

MAGIC YOU CAN TOUCH

'Steven, time to get up. I need a hand please.' My Nana Lynne's broad Bradford accent boomed outside my bedroom door just as dawn was breaking. Blearily opening my eyes, I checked the alarm clock: 5.45 a.m. I could hear the dogs barking already from the kennels down the back of the garden. I groaned and went back to sleep.

If you've ever wondered what living with nineteen dogs is like, I can tell you: smelly, loud and hairy. When I asked my Nana Lynne if I could stay in America with her for a few months, I had no idea what I was letting myself in for.

She had moved to Memphis with her new husband, Martin, a few years before and set up her own dog-breeding business. A champion dog breeder, my Nana Lynne has nineteen award-winning Golden Retrievers. She travels across the US from state to state in her purpose-built Winnebago, doing all of the major dog shows. As I had decided to defer my place at college for a year, I thought it would be a good experience for me to hang out in America for a bit. Although I'd pictured Disneyland and supersized fast food, I got dog shows and Pedigree Chum.

Dog breeding is competitive, but rather than, say, Crufts, the dog shows my grandma competes in are more about demonstrating the standard of your dog breeding. So although there are obedience tests and obstacle courses, the focus is on the quality of the dogs themselves. And there is rather more at stake than a rosette, as winning ultimately means you can charge more money for your dogs. Whether you breed Chihuahuas or Bulldogs, the more competitions you win, the more your dogs are worth. My Nana's dogs have won countless awards and have even been in television adverts for things like Pedigree Chum. They are amazing.

Dog shows are a serious business and they take a lot of preparation. We'd wake up early in the morning, feed and water Nana Lynne's nineteen Golden Retrievers, take them for long walks, groom them and train them for the shows. After our own breakfast, we'd jump in the Winnebago and roll to wherever the dog show was that day. One way or another, I was constantly covered in dog hair. Before then, I'd never been the biggest animal lover but after that I can appreciate why people are so attached to them. They're such loving, loyal creatures.

While it might have been hairy and hard work, the experience would unwittingly yet profoundly change my approach to magic. Once again magic seemed to find me... When I wasn't running around with dogs, or chilling with my grandparents, I was, as ever, obsessively working on my magic. Back home, I'd been getting those bookings most weekends. I was securing by financially and, slowly, my name was starting to gain some momentum, if only in local magic circles. But magic never seemed like a realistic career. I had no idea that I could make it a full-time job; as far as I was concerned, I was having a year in the US then I'd return home, go to college, and get a 'real' job. As it turned out, I never went back to college.

Following each dog show there would be an 'after-party' of sorts. It might not have been Jay-Z's idea of VIP, but among the tea and sandwiches, it turned out that people were always up for checking out the magic that a little English kid had to offer. The word among the dog circles spread and I performed in tents after the dog shows. I even visited the infamous Magic Castle in LA, an exclusive magic members club, where I saw lots of jobbing magicians who appeared to be making a decent living. It helped to make me see the possibility that a career in magic might not be such a daft idea. If all these guys could do it, maybe I had a shot.

♠

When I first went to the US, Nana and Martin were living in Virginia. After a couple of weeks, we moved to Memphis where there were more opportunities for dog breeders. I can't say that I got to see loads of the city. I didn't know any kids my own age and Nana Lynne wasn't about to go out raving all night with me. But from what I did get to see, Memphis was a great city. It's down in the South, in Tennessee, so it's all slow talking, soul food and sweaty summers. It also has an incredible musical heritage. Everyone from Elvis to Johnny Cash and Justin Timberlake grew up in the city, and to this day you can always find a bar or club, day or night, pumping out live music.

A lot of magicians played in the city too. Being in Memphis was really the first time that I saw other people do magic. Over the years, I'd watched Gramps, but I didn't go out and watch magic. I'd read practical magic books, but I had very little knowledge of the history of the art. It didn't seem relevant to the type of magic that I was interested in. One day, Grandpa got us tickets to see David Copperfield film a TV special. Copperfield is renowned for his extravagant sets and I remember being blown away not only by the scale and spectacle, but also by his incredibly compelling stage persona. It was amazing. On a whole different level.

I bought the DVD box set at the end of the night, which was a compilation of Copperfield's greatest moments. It showed me how vast his career was and how far he took magic. This is the guy who has made the Statue of Liberty disappear, who levitated over the Grand Canyon, and who walked through the middle of the Great Wall of China, not to mention sawing Claudia Schiffer in half. I had huge respect for David Copperfield, but for me, a working-class kid from Bradford, his world of magic seemed so far from mine. I didn't want a glamorous assistant and a suit; I wanted to do close-up magic wearing my trainers and cap. But who would be interested in that?

While I was in Memphis, I heard that Daryl the Magician was coming to town. Daryl is a legend and an absolute genius. He was the World Champion Card Magician at FISM (Fédération Internationale des Sociétés Magiques), which is like the Olympics of magic. He has won every magic award that's ever been created, and he continues to work as a creative magic consultant. He made his money from owning the company that makes and distributes 90 per cent of fancy-dress costumes in America. He was already rich, so for him magic was never about the money: it was his passion.

A friend of mine who was part of the Memphis Magic Ring had invited Daryl to talk at a magic night he had just started up. He rang me excitedly to tell me the news. 'The problem is, Steven, it's at a nightclub, so it's for twenty-one-year-olds and over. I don't think you have much hope for passing for eighteen, let alone twenty-one.'

I was gutted that Daryl was going to be in Memphis and I couldn't go and see him.

The next day, I had to get up super early. It was just after seven when Nana and I left her house and got in the car. She'd asked

me to go with her to someone's house to help them with their dogs. She would drop me off, I'd do some training with them, and she'd be back later to pick me up.

It turned out to be the house of the person who'd flown Daryl to Memphis for the lecture. My Nana Lynne had known all along; it was her special surprise to me because I hadn't been able to go to the show.

'All right, mate, how you doing?' This was my cocky greeting when I saw Daryl sat at the breakfast table. I was a confident kid back then, I had no fear. When I told him that I too was a magician, Daryl grinned and invited me to sit down and have breakfast. I've been friends with him ever since. I don't speak to him regularly, but whenever I do, I always get so much from our conversations.

Daryl taught me about the art of show business and how to show and tell without saying anything at all. Obviously his secrets are his trade, the same as my secrets are my trade. He taught me how to keep that mystery, whilst still being forthcoming. Daryl is one of those really clever people who never actually gives you anything or teaches you anything, but he'll speak to you and explain things to you and look at you very meaningfully. You go away feeling like you've gained something, even if you don't know exactly what it is. An hour in his company is enlightening and inspirational. He also taught me that magicians don't have to be full of themselves. You can be cool and down to earth while still putting on a show. He told me he could see no reason why I wouldn't be able to make it. 'Just do what you're doing and you'll get there.' It filled me with confidence to know that I was doing the right thing by being myself.

While I was in Memphis, we had a trip to New Orleans that would further change my perspective on magic. My uncle was also visiting America at the time; he owns the biggest diving warehouse in the world and they make the best wetsuits. He was going to a diving conference in New Orleans, so my Nana Lynne and Martin and I drove there to meet up with him.

'Stay close, Steven, and don't look at anyone,' Martin said, grabbing my arm as we crossed Bourbon Street. I was eighteen years old. This was the uncoolest thing ever. I tried to shake my granddad loose but he wasn't having it.

New Orleans back in the nineties was quite scary. This was before Hurricane Katrina, before they tried to regenerate the city. For those into hip hop, this was the time of Soulja Slim, a young Lil Wayne and a fledgling Cash Money. It was also the murder capital of the USA; around the time I was there, there were around 400 murders a year. Everywhere you went, there were crowds of people: tourists, blaggers, gangstas, bums and hustlers.

We walked down Bourbon Street and found my uncle with some colleagues enjoying a beer in one of the many bars that lined the street. 'Someone was stabbed in here last night,' his friend said casually, as everyone shrugged and ordered their drinks.

I was spooked; everyone was carrying on as if this were a normal occurrence. I realised pretty quickly that in New Orleans, violence was a way of life. All I heard was 'Stand next to your granddad, Steven'; 'Where are you going? Stay with us'; 'I'll come with you'. My family was very overcautious with me, making sure that I kept close to them all the time. I wasn't even allowed to go to the toilet on my own – they'd wait outside the cubicle. It just seemed odd, and I felt slightly on edge because they were acting out of the ordinary.

Looking back now, I think it's one of the most amazing places I've ever been to. New Orleans is a very magical, mystical city. Voodoo has been a part of New Orleans for over two centuries and there are a number of historical shops, museums and cemeteries. I want to go back there – I think it would be an interesting place to perform.

The most fascinating part of being in New Orleans, for me, was seeing street magicians do their thing. Everywhere you looked, people were hustling on the streets. This was the kind of magic Gramps had shown me, but it was out in the real world; this was the type of magic that made total sense to me. It brought magic directly into people's lives, right there, in front of their eyes. It was magic you could touch.

I would see street magicians of all ages do incredible things with everyday objects; they'd perform close-up card magic, make flowers disappear and do the most incredible things with balloons. They were so quick. And they would make a killing from willing punters eager to place a bet on where a card or flower might end up next.

Before then, I was probably conforming a little bit more to what I thought a typical magician might do, like cup and ball routines; I was working on an act that had to be done in a specific setting, thinking along more traditional, linear lines. Being in New Orleans changed everything I thought I knew about magic. I didn't realise that you could just do any type of magic anywhere. I didn't have the mindset then, that if you could really do magic, you just do it. You don't need a fancy set with smoke and mirrors – all you need is yourself and the spectator. In later years I would disregard having anything like a cup and ball routine or any type of props as such. While I always travel with my cards, I prefer to improvise with what is around me. People's watches, phones, a drink can, an old piece of wire, snow... it doesn't matter what it is, I'll always find some way to create something astonishing out of nothing. Whenever I do magic, whether it's a booking, in front of my mates or even, sometimes, when filming my TV show, I love the art of the unexpected; I can even surprise myself sometimes.

♠

Over time, I realised the importance of knowing what your peers are doing. You can't live in a world where only you and your magic exist; how can you learn and grow from that?

But while I may study other people's concepts, I'll always change them and make them my own. I'll look at what someone's done and take it to the next level: magicians may have walked on water before, but never on a body of water as dangerous as the Thames. I've admired and learnt from magicians including Houdini and David Blaine, and there are many magicians that I've been lucky enough to meet along the way who have added to my experiences, ideas and style.

Many people think magic started with Houdini, the infamous escapologist. Yet you can trace magic back to the dawn of time; it was probably called something else in those days. If you look at the drawings that cavemen used to do, there was certainly an element of mysticism in those paintings. Having a sense of wonderment, and questioning what is and isn't possible, is, I think, an inherent part of human nature.

Recorded magic is as old as history itself. Around 5,000 years ago, a common man called Dedi was summoned to the palace of an Egyptian pharaoh called Cheops. Dedi was thought to be 110 years old and survived on 100 jars of beer, a shoulder of beef and 500 loaves of bread a day. After arriving at the palace, he was asked to perform the magic he was famous for – decapitation. He grabbed a goose, a pelican and an ox, and, in turn, pulled off each of their heads with his bare hands. Once the stunned crowd had ascertained each animal was dead, Dedi picked up the head, took it back to the now-lifeless body and stuck it back on. Each animal immediately squawked back to life, running around the palace, much to the delight of the pharaoh and his subjects.

You can imagine his thoughts when the king asked him to perform the magic again on a prisoner. I'm not sure how he wangled himself out of that one...!

Throughout time and through many civilisations, from ancient Greece and Rome to medieval England, magicians have been a crucial part of society. Back then when there was no television, cinema, computer games, Twitter or BlackBerry, people had to make their own entertainment. Whether that was William Shakespeare entertaining the masses at the Globe, or the likes of the court jester amusing the Queen and her subjects, people have always wanted to be amazed and entertained.

It was around the nineteenth century that magic really changed. Before then, it had been the domain of the very poor or the very rich, taking place either in palaces or sewage-filled market squares. The middle classes sneered at magic, believing it to be for the simple and poor or the rich and bored. But then a Frenchman called Jean Eugène Robert-Houdin swapped the wizard cloaks for a top hat and tails. Robert-Houdin took magic to the theatre, giving it a physical home and a broader audience. Robert-Houdin was known for some incredible magic – most famously catching a bullet between his teeth. Magic had earned a newfound respect, finally beginning to shake off the stereotypes of 'witchcraft and wizardry'.

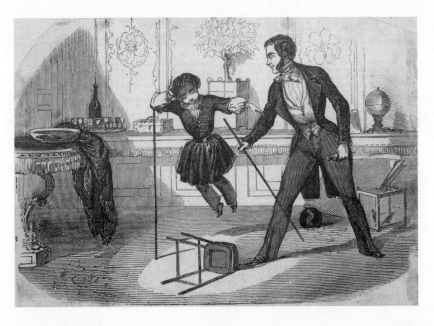

After Robert-Houdin came the almighty Harry Houdini, who would go on to become one of magic's most famous practitioners. Still widely regarded as the greatest ever escapologist, stunt artist, showman and magician of all time, Houdini awed millions of people all over the world during the late 1800s and early 1900s. He escaped from a straitjacket while being dangled upside-down from a crane one hundred feet in the air. He freed himself from an airtight case at the bottom of a swimming pool. Manacled in a lead-encased crate, he was lowered into New York's East River and escaped in just fifty-seven seconds. There was always a new challenge that Houdini was willing to try.

Houdini eventually died in 1926 after receiving a series of blows to the abdomen by a university student named J. Gordon Whitehead. Whitehead had asked Houdini if it was true that he could take any amount of punches to the stomach, to which Houdini, lying down on a couch at the time, had replied yes. Houdini stood up, but before he had time to prepare himself properly, it is said that Whitehead unexpectedly hit him three times in the stomach. Already ill with a ruptured appendix,

HARRY HOUDINI
THE JAIL BREAKER
INTRODUCING HIS LATEST & GREATEST
PRISON CELL & BARREL MYSTERY
HOUDINI is strapped & locked in a barrel placed in a police cell which is also locked and in less than 2 seconds changes places.
£100. WILL BE PAID TO ANYONE FINDING TRAPS, PANELS OR FALSE DOORS IN THE CELL

he continued to perform but died a couple of weeks later on 31 October of peritonitis. He was fifty-two years old.

Through Houdini, and others like Robert-Houdin, David Copperfield and Siegfried & Roy, magic became a legitimate art form, as revered by society as music, painting or sportsmanship. There's a reason why David Copperfield is one of the top ten highest-paid celebrities worldwide. This guy stood in the centre of a 'tornado of fire'. He escaped from Alcatraz. He made NASA angry when he made the moon vanish for four seconds. You don't get to play to the amount of people that Copperfield has and make the money he has made by being 'quite good'. And he is not the only master of his trade. Penn and Teller might have a very different style to Copperfield, or indeed to me, but they are without question the best magic duo out there. They are constantly reinventing what magic is and I respect them greatly for that.

The entire history of magic is really a whole other story, but I wanted to give a little insight into how it all happened because, as I always say, if you don't know where you've been, how do you know where you're going?

In those early years, I had a lot of lessons to learn, and it's because of meeting people like Daryl the Magician that I was able to hone my magic and start to see success. As well as observing Gramps, I soaked up ideas from the street performers in New Orleans and other professionals like Lee Asher, Mac King and Wayne Dobson. They may not be household names, but within the world of magic, they're respected by the best.

That's what I learnt during my time in America that year. I went with the idea that magic would be a lifetime hobby; I left with the knowledge and the knowhow to turn it into a career. I guess I should be thankful to those Golden Retrievers!

CHAPTER 4

AVOIDING THE STRAIGHT LINES

While I was in Memphis, I made a decision. I was going to move to Las Vegas, the home of magic. I'd seen how the likes of Daryl the Magician had built their careers and I was inspired. I'd had such good feedback from doing the dog shows and the odd performance in Memphis that I felt confident I could make my name in Vegas. My vague, some might say insane, plan was that word of mouth would spread and my own television show would soon follow. Simple.

I returned home and formulated a plan. I would get myself a gaming licence so that I could work in Vegas when I turned twenty-one. I figured that I'd get a licence in Bradford, sort out a placement in Vegas and then pursue my career in magic, but have the licence to fall back on if anything went wrong.

I got myself a trainee position working as a croupier for Gala Bingo in Bradford. A croupier is someone who works in a casino on everything from the blackjack table to the roulette wheel. I would take people's bets as well as working out what they'd won.

I'd always been pretty good at maths, which is essential in the job, and I spent a lot of time adding and multiplying at scarily fast rates. I didn't realise it at the time, but thinking fast on my feet would bode well in later years; particularly when it came to

doing predictions. Being able to work out the odds of something quickly is not a bad skill to have in my line of work.

This being Bradford, it wasn't all glitz and glamour; there was no Sharon Stone lounging half-naked over the Texas Hold'em table and James Bond swilling his specially shaken Martini. It was working-class people standing on gaudy carpet with bright overhead lights, lots of late nights, and because it was before the smoking ban, the club would be full of clouds of B&H as punters puffed away over the tables. I'd leave in the early hours of the morning, physically and mentally exhausted, stinking of smoke, sweat and the spilt drinks of customers who'd gotten carried away with the booze.

Despite all that, I enjoyed the work. I was always busy and it was well paid and I had a goal in mind. I was working towards something and as I saw my savings slowly increase, it gave me even more impetus to work long, unsociable hours. My boys may have been out partying, but I couldn't let that be my life at that point; I needed to stay focused on my goals: a licence and Las Vegas.

I managed to save a couple of thousand pounds quite quickly and, a few months later, I had enough money to take a short holiday to the infamous Sin City. I landed at dusk, and because the airport is so close to the main strip I could see the sun setting over the 'Eiffel Tower', the 'Pyramids' and the 'Statue of Liberty'. The lights of Vegas are so bright, you can see them from space. As I left the airport terminal to jump in a cab, the view of the city as it turned from dusk to evening was pretty magical.

It's no surprise that magic does such big business in this city: it's loud, brash and full of empty promises and broken dreams. When you've lost your life savings on the roulette wheel or the blackjack table, you're going to want to see something that gives you hope. In some ways, Vegas is the home of magic. It's where all the main players 'retire' to when they're ready to do a few years of shows and make their millions on the constant stream of audiences that pour into the city each day.

I've met some of the most interesting magicians in Vegas, and it's also a place where I have learnt the most about magic – not from watching it, necessarily, but from listening and talking to other magicians who are masters of their trade.

On that first trip, for example, I finally got to see Apollo Robbins, one of the world's most famous pickpockets. He describes himself as a 'gentleman thief'. He was the first person I met who really understood the power of communication.

He worked in Vegas as a host at Caesar's Magical Empire; he was the guy who greeted everyone before they had dinner and took them through to the dining room. It was quite amazing to see; all these unsuspecting diners who suddenly found their watch, wallet and phone in the hands of the mischievous host. Obviously he returned everything at the end!

When the former US President Jimmy Carter went to Caesar's for dinner, Robbins was told he was allowed to do anything, apart from touch the President; so he stole every single gun from the Secret Service, the President's security detail. Not long after, he was asked to work as a security consultant for various law enforcement firms.

I didn't meet him that time, but later in the year we were both at a conference in Vegas. I managed to sidle up to him and we started chatting. We immediately got on and he invited me to a nearby twenty-four-hour diner, where he really broke the art of magic down for me.

'People follow straight lines, they don't follow curves,' he told me. I didn't know what he meant at first, but he continued. 'When I'm onstage, if I want to do something, but I don't want people to see it, I use an arc with my hand because people are less likely to notice anything. Because there's no straight line, there's nothing for them to follow. If you're doing anything as a straight line, and there's an off moment, people will notice it.' His analogy was much better – it made a lot more sense! But it was an invaluable lesson; using an arc and avoiding a straight line, literally and metaphorically, is key in magic.

We talked for ages after his show. He, I, and a few other magicians just sat in the diner until six in the morning, talking. It was the first conversation I'd had with people about magic where it wasn't about the 'tricks'. That's when I really started to understand that it's about the people you're performing for, and the way you communicate with them. Those magicians in Vegas showed me about the power of showmanship and stage presence, the kind of things that you attribute to superstars like Michael Jackson. There are so many things that Michael did which are now synonymous with him – like the Moonwalk for example. He didn't start off doing that, he wasn't born knowing how to do it; it's something he created and then practised and practised until he made it seem effortless.

It really made me think about my approach to magic. I realised that I don't perform magic; what you see and how your mind perceives it is the magic. Magic only happens in the spectator's mind. I'm presenting what I do in a certain way, but without the spectator there is no magic. Without them, it simply doesn't exist.

Another thing that I learnt was that I don't really believe in 'magic' as such, which I know sounds weird. I don't believe magic exists as a 'thing' at all; to me it's more a physical feeling and emotion that you get when you see something that you can't explain. When you're a baby, you have no idea how anything works, so everything's magical.

The greatest magic I've ever experienced will always be at Gramps' house. But some of the best lessons I've learnt have been on the streets of New Orleans, over breakfast in Memphis and in twenty-four-hour diners in Las Vegas.

♠

I'd always imagined that some day I'd end up in Las Vegas with my own show. But after that first visit, I decided that actually, Las Vegas wasn't the place for me. I didn't want to be stuck out there for a long period of time and I didn't really want to be on a stage performing. I wanted to be on the streets, amongst my audience.

But I still travelled to Vegas for the odd visit. The more I went and the more magicians I met there, the more it made me re-evaluate my approach and the direction I wanted to take with my magic. I wasn't like any of those guys with their big stage shows and incredible props. I didn't have a suit and tie and there were no lions involved in my act. But meeting people like Apollo and Daryl, I saw that I didn't need to follow the herd. Being myself was actually the greatest strength I had. When I started out, there was certainly no one else like me. I was a young kid from the North of England who, like most teenagers, liked music, video games, films and girls. And that was a great thing. Kids my own age related to me, and people who were older than me were intrigued to see magic done, live, in the street in front of them rather than from via television where they might suspect trickery.

Being different was the best thing about me; in many ways it was one of my main strengths and it would help me a great deal in those early years.

Although I didn't move to Vegas, the money I saved as a croupier helped me to start my own business. The city did help me begin a professional career, just not in the way that I had expected. With my savings, I would travel around Leeds, Manchester and Bradford, making links in the music and television industries. I started to turn up at hip-hop shows where artists like Ms. Dynamite and Jazzy Jeff would perform on tour. I started to put together pamphlets, quotes and clips that would eventually end up on my first DVD.

While Vegas might not have been right for me as a magician early on in my career, maybe one day I'll end up there. I have lots of ideas for my live show, but I want to really think about it

properly before I do it, so that it's the best live magic show anyone has ever seen. That's when I'll know that I've really made it. When I can sell out a few months at Caesar's, I'll finally pat myself on the back and say, '*Yes, Dynamo. You did it.*'

♠

While I'm not ready as yet to have a live show in Vegas, I have experimented with theatre in the past.

In 2007, I did a live show in London. At that point, I'd had some success, but I still didn't have my own television show. So, as a sort of business card, I decided to create a live show at the Soho Theatre to which I could invite friends, family and members of the industry. It was very stripped back and low-key – it was about as far from Vegas as you can get.

After the short run of five nights, to my utter amazement, Kevin Spacey invited me to the Old Vic to perform it for him. He had seen me do my magic at a Prince's Trust event a couple of years before and really liked it. I had various corporate companies interested in booking me as a live performer, so he offered to help me condense the one-hour show into a twenty-minute capsule that would work in the corporate world.

As the lights went up, I could see him in the audience and, if that wasn't pressure enough, the actor Jeff Goldblum was sat right beside him. No pressure.

Trying to translate the close-up magic I do into live theatre turned out to be a lot tougher than I had anticipated. The whole show was based around me interacting with a television screen, and before I'd barely begun, the scart lead decided to break. Not the best start! After that, everything seemed to go wrong and I could see Kevin furiously scribbling notes throughout.

Afterwards, Kevin took me into his office and told me straight: 'This doesn't work'. Admittedly, it was tough to take such straightforward criticism, especially from an actor and director that I admired, but it was what I needed to hear. The show was terrible!

Back then, being on stage wasn't my forte. I'd always been a close-up, street performer so I didn't know about projecting my voice or turning my body out towards the audience. Kevin gave me some great tips and he hooked me up with a drama teacher to help me figure out how to use the space on stage better and how to project my voice from my diaphragm rather than my throat.

Not only did he give me his time, Kevin also invited me to join a workshop with final-year students from RADA. The workshop taught me that you have to live outside yourself when you're in front of an audience – you've got to lose your ego and not be too self-conscious if you want to give yourself in a performance. You've got to be in the moment as a performer. It can be hard for me – for anybody – to really expose myself like that. You may have a huge amount going on in your private life, you may feel ill that day, or you may just be in a bad mood. But onstage, you have to learn to handle your emotions and control what people see.

It was such a great learning curve. The idea had been well-intentioned but I quickly realised that I shouldn't put anything out– even if just for friends and family – that I wasn't completely confident in. I really appreciate that Kevin took the time out to explain where I was going wrong. It's still something I'm working on, to be honest, but I hope I'll be able to do a live show with more success very soon. I have a lot of ideas and I have the advice from Kevin to guide me. It will happen one day.

CHAPTER 5

THE
HEROES
OF MAGIC

I was nineteen the first time I went to New York. I arrived in the Big Apple as 'Steven, the-Hip-Hop-Magician-Kid-from-Bradford' and left not only with the respect of my peers, but also with a brand-new name.

It was 2001, and I had been invited by the International Brotherhood of Magicians (IBM) and the Society of American Magicians (SAM) to attend a four-day conference. It was, as usual with anything magic-related, shrouded in secrecy, so I can't reveal too much. What I can say is that ordinarily, there are two separate magic conferences a year that take place in different parts of America. Because it was the centenary of the SAM, founded by the great Harry Houdini, the society had decided to team up with the IBM for the first time and hold a joint conference in New York as a celebration of the release of their joint Houdini commemorative stamp. It's essentially a conference similar to that which you might get for music, art or business – but for magic. There are talks, seminars, demonstrations and shows. Because the IBM and the SAM had joined up this particular year, I knew that the cream of the crop would be descending on New York for those four days. I figured if I could get myself a spot performing there, it could have a great impact on my career.

if you have a dream, then New York is the place to make it come true

I wangled an invite through a magician friend who I'd met on holiday in Las Vegas earlier that year. Although I was welcome to attend, I would have to pay my own way out there. Luckily, even though I was young, I was doing OK and had built up some savings through my croupier job in the casino in Bradford. I made £795 a month and, living rent-free with my great-grandparents, I either ate Nana's cooking (which was the best in the world) or had free meals at work because I worked nights. I didn't drink, I didn't smoke, and I didn't have a phone bill because no one had mobile phones back then. On the rare occasions I had to buy myself food, I'd go to my favourite curry house in Bradford, where you could get a meal for two for £5. It was almost impossible for me to get rid of my money so I was saving around £600 a month. Not only did I not have anything to spend my wages on, but also I made sure I saved because I had a goal in mind, an ambition to achieve.

I went to America four times that year alone, paid for by myself. I would go to Las Vegas to see the latest developments in the magic shows; I'd pop to LA for the odd gig and, towards the end of 2001, I took the opportunity to go to New York.

♠

Getting on the plane I felt a nervous rumble. I'd been to America before to visit my grandma in Memphis, and hung out in Vegas with my magician friends. But this was different. Besides the fact that it was it a huge city with a formidable reputation that I'd never been to before, I'd also be going on my own.

I might have been anxious, but as I boarded the flight, I had a funny feeling that things would be OK. New York was the birthplace of hip hop and it was the setting for some of film's most iconic moments. Many of my favourite rappers, actors and film directors hailed from the place they called the Big Apple. I couldn't wait to take a bite.

As the jumbo jet landed in New York, I glimpsed the city through the smog. It looked tiny from the plane and I wondered if it would live up to my huge expectations.

I collected my bags and jumped in a taxi into town. The cab sped through Queens and the nerves returned; the area looked quite rough. There were huge project buildings, run-down shops and dubious-looking people hanging out on the corners. Who knows, perhaps I passed a young 50 Cent up to no good on those mean streets! My butterflies increased tenfold.

When the taxi finally hit Manhattan after about an hour, the contrast was remarkable. We passed Grand Central Station and crawled through the rush-hour traffic. It was mind-blowing, like something out of a film. Huge buildings towered above me, yellow cabs honked their horns at the thousands of people hurrying past, their focus firmly fixed on whatever important destination they were headed to. I looked to my left and could just about see the Empire State Building. As a film fanatic, it felt weird to see these iconic landmarks in real life. New York was like one big movie set.

Although I've been to New York a lot of times now, I still have the same funny feeling when I first land there. It's like anything is possible in that city; if you have a dream, then New York is the place to try and live it. Its energy is like nowhere else. The city truly never sleeps!

♠

I had done my research before going to New York and discovered that you could stay cheaply at the Hilton Hotel, where the magic conference was being held, if you were prepared to share with someone else.

My roommate was a tall ginger guy whose name I have since forgotten, and his assistant, who was also his girlfriend. It was a bit awkward, sharing a room with a couple, but we rarely saw each other. My roommate and his girlfriend had an act called the Quick Change where they would dance and do twenty outfit changes in three minutes. He would throw glitter in the air and the next thing you knew, her red dress would be changed to a glittery one. It was made famous by David and Dania, who did it on *America's Got Talent*. It was a real eye-opener to share our ideas of magic and to be amongst all that creativity. Lying back on my bed the first night, I was excited about getting to the conference the following morning. I was looking forward to being exposed to new thoughts and the greatest magic I had ever seen. My stomach fluttered with anticipation.

As I had hoped, it was amazing. On the first day I saw Siegfried and Roy and watched a magnetic David Copperfield deliver a seminar about his life in magic; how he had fallen in love with magic as a little boy.

I was so busy running about meeting people I barely got time to see much of the city. I just about managed to visit Times Square, and the only places I went were within walking distance of the Hilton, which was on the Avenue of the Americas where all the skyscrapers are. Looking up at them, towering above me, memories of Spider-Man leaping from rooftop to rooftop and scaling down the sides of huge buildings came back to me. Finally, I was living in the movies – just like I'd always wanted to.

There were 2,000 magicians at the conference, so I made lots of friends, many of whom I'm still in touch with. It was the ultimate networking spot for magicians. I got to know an escapologist called Spencer Horseman, who was from New York, and a girl who, it turned out, was Houdini's great-great-great-niece. Spencer was also recently featured on *America's Got Talent*. Me, him and Houdini's distant relation would go out each night when the conference was finished and find pizza on the not-so-mean streets of uptown Manhattan.

Coming from Bradford, where I was the only person that I knew doing magic, it was a revelation to meet people my own age who were into the same things. For the first time ever, I felt like I really belonged. We might have all been misfits in whatever town we had grown up in, but here, we were all like-minded individuals interested only in the pursuit of bigger and better magic.

♠

I had never felt pressure like it. I might have been in the anonymous surroundings of a beige and brown conference room in New York, but I was encircled by magic's most famous practitioners. David Blaine leant expectantly against a wall, while Aaron Fisher, a highly respected sleight-of-hand manipulator, jostled for space alongside Paul Wilson, the magician from BBC3's *The Real Hustle*. We had gathered together to share our particular style of magic with each other.

As a musician or actor can testify, there's nothing tougher than performing in front of your peers. Here I was, a teenager from Bradford with half-baked ideas about being a magician, surrounded by a 'who's who' of modern magic. What had I got myself into?

As the host introduced me, I looked around the room at the gathered greats and pulled myself together. This could be my big break and I wasn't about to blow it. I delved deep inside and went for it. The first thing I did was make coins disappear and reappear in people's pockets, under watches and even under someone's hat. It drew murmurs of appreciation, my next illusion, a gasp or two. As I grew in confidence, my magic got better and better. I was good, and I knew it. I had spent the last six years obsessively practising in my bedroom, waiting for an opportunity like this. The crowd may have been a hard one, but I was more than ready for them.

I felt Blaine lean forward as the buzz in the room began to grow. I paused to ready my recently invented card shuffle, inspired by the breakdancers of this very city. It was a risky strategy because, back then, I didn't always pull it off. I danced with the deck, the cards coming to life in my hands before I stacked them on top of each other so that they came to rest perfectly on my cap.

'This kid's a f***king dynamo!' a voice shouted from the fifty or so gathered greats. '*Dynamo*?' I thought, but quickly dismissed it because, to be honest, I didn't really know what it meant. I thought it was just some American slang word.

It was about a year later, when I finally turned professional, that I looked up the word in the dictionary. It said, 'A small generator that gives massive electrifying results.' It couldn't have summed me up any better. I might be small, but I like to think my performances are larger than life. I still don't know who shouted it out, but both Aaron Fisher and Paul Wilson claim to be the person who inadvertently named me that day. Apparently, before I had

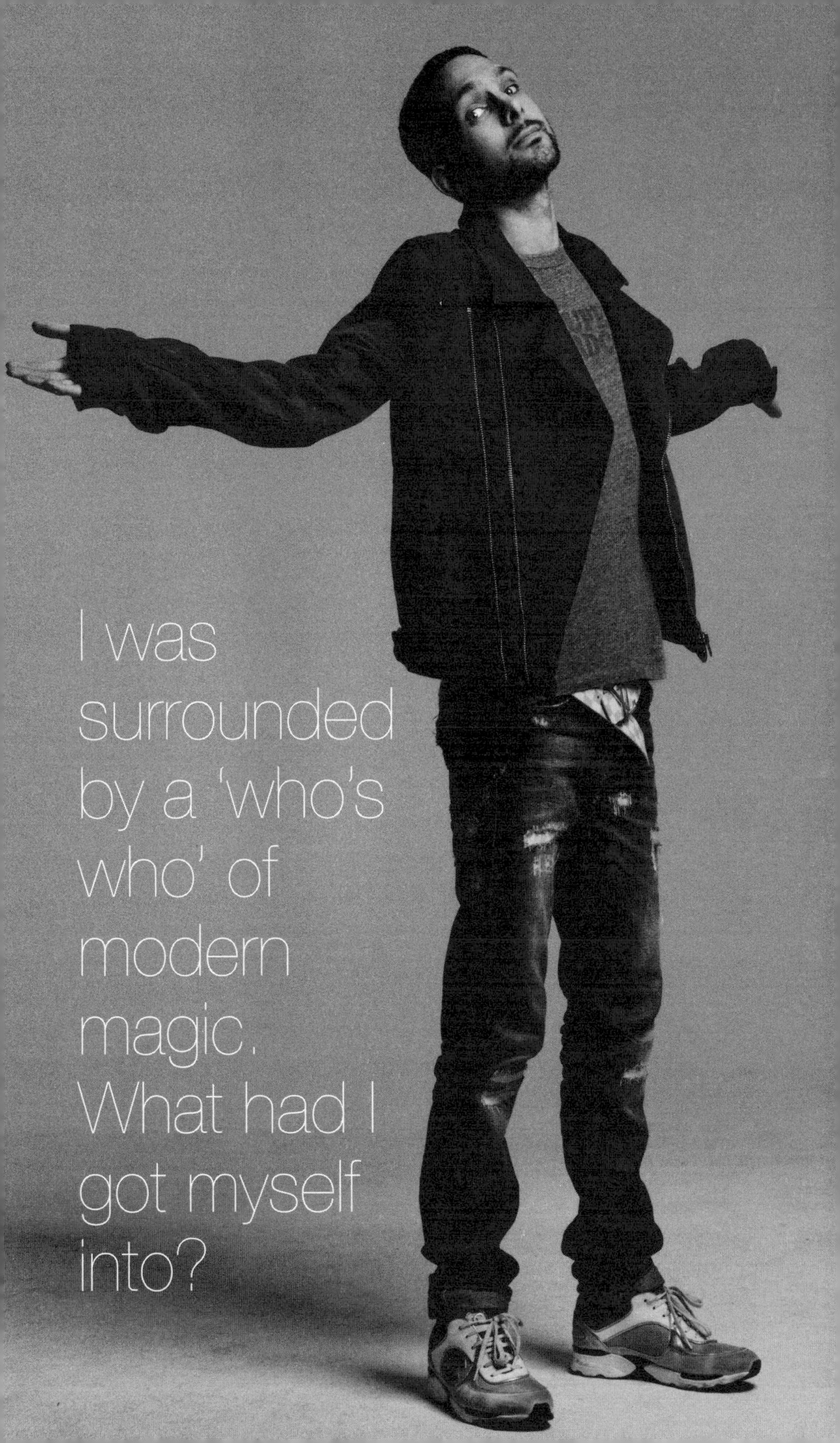

I was
surrounded
by a 'who's
who' of
modern
magic.
What had I
got myself
into?

met Aaron, Paul had described me to him, saying, 'The kid is like a dynamo.' Aaron insists that he was the one to shout it out that day.

They're both good friends of mine now, so whoever wants to take the credit, I thank you!

♠

While I was at the centenary celebrations, I got to meet David Copperfield's assistant and a few of his people, though I didn't meet the man himself on that trip. A year or so later, I went back to Vegas and connected with Chris Kenner, who is Copperfield's business partner and right-hand man. Even though I wouldn't see the man himself again, Chris still had some great plans up his sleeve. 'So, do you want to come to Copperfield's place?' he asked. David wouldn't actually be there, but I decided that just hanging out in the great man's lair would be insightful enough for me. I bet you could absorb the magic by osmosis! I jumped at the chance.

To me, David Copperfield is like the Michael Jackson of magic. Copperfield was from the same era as Michael and they are both on a level as performers – true entertainers. Copperfield has won the most awards and has sold more tickets to his own shows than anyone else in the world, ever. He still does over 500 shows a year, sometimes performing two in one night. His wealth is vast; he owns eleven islands and is the world's largest private collector of magical artefacts.

Although I'd never felt inclined to be like Copperfield in terms of the style of magic that I do, I was certainly inspired by the manner in which he had achieved such greatness. His love for magic was so obvious. It had never been about the money, power and fame for him; that was just a by-product of his hard work, determination and passion for magic.

I didn't need to be asked twice to experience a glimpse inside the mind of one of the greatest entertainers of the twenty-first century, so, along with a couple of people, including Danny Garcia, a magician who now works closely with me and who I had met at a conference in Vegas, we arranged to meet Kenner later that evening.

We arrived at a very nondescript-looking street, on the outskirts of Sin City, and all we could see were lots of warehouses. Kenner was waiting for us outside a bra shop, of all places. 'Welcome, everybody,' he said, ushering us in through the doors of the lingerie emporium. It turned out that in order to enter Copperfield's cavern, you had to walk through the lingerie store. When you leave, everyone who has been invited to David's studio is given a mug from the bra shop! Only those who are in the know, know. I still have that cup in my kitchen today.

We walked through the store, bras and topless mannequins everywhere, until we came to a door. Like the back of the wardrobe leading to Narnia, the entrance opened up into a magician's box of delights.

Everywhere I looked in the cavernous warehouse were antique posters, original artwork, letters from Houdini, Houdini's straitjacket, incredible props that had been used by the greats over the years, as well as vast sets from Copperfield's elaborate shows. What was apparent was how deep his love and respect, for magic went. Going to the warehouse inspired me to read up much more on the history of magic. I don't know that I'd pass a GCSE in it today, but I left there determined to find out much more about my chosen career.

I finally met the man himself in 2012 when he invited me to see his show in Las Vegas. My friend and I were given front-row seats and treated like royalty. 'Thanks so much for coming,' he said when we were introduced after the show, his blue eyes as piercing as I had imagined. It's funny, people always say that I have unusual eyes too; perhaps it's the sign of a great magician! 'Thank you also for telling your Twitter followers,' he continued.

Apparently they'd had a spike in British bookings because I'd tweeted that I was going. It was just after *Dynamo: Magician Impossible* had been on in America, and I had around 250,000 followers on Twitter. We took a picture together and he not only tweeted me, but he also tweeted links to some clips of my show online. I could only hope to be so gracious and charming when I've been in the game for as long as he has.

Never in a million years would I have pictured meeting David Copperfield, let alone winning his respect.

♠

Whenever I've met one of my heroes, it often seems to have happened by chance. Maybe us magicians are all cosmically connected in some weird way? Back in New York, at the Hilton Hotel where I was staying for the conference, I was standing outside when I heard the screech of tyres and the gasp of the crowd. 'Is that David Blaine?' squealed a tourist who happened to be passing by.

I looked to where everyone was pointing as Blaine skidded up on his motorbike. His show, *Street Magic*, had been on American television for about a year and he was a total and utter rock star back then. Dressed head to toe in black leather, he got off this gigantic Harley, helping his passenger – the actress, Daryl Hannah – to dismount. I looked at him in awe – not only was he a famous and respected magician, but he had a hot actress on his arm too. My eyes and mouth were wide open.

'David, David, can I get a picture?' Everyone was hassling him for a photo, but I decided to try something a little more subtle. I'd already impressed him with my magic back in the Hilton's stuffy conference room; here was my chance to show him I was always ready and waiting. He spotted me doing my special shuffle and laughed. 'OK, kid, let's see what you got today,' he grinned. I showed him something new that I was working on, involving a series of complex card effects that he seemed impressed by. He called over his rock star-style friends who were waiting for him in the hotel lobby. 'Man, this kid's good,' he said in his deep rumble, shaking his head. 'He really knows what he is doing.' Years later, he kindly allowed me to use those very words on the cover of my first DVD, *Underground Magic*.

And those words will stay with me forever too. For him to say something like that about me was an incredible moment. Like magic, I found it hard to believe.

On that first trip to New York, I not only found my name, but I also learnt that real magic comes from the heart. Without passion and self-belief, I could end up like any of the other thousands of struggling magicians out there. Instead, while everyone else stood around taking pictures of Blaine, I did what I had gone to New York to do: learn the art of magic.

CHAPTER 6

REMEMBER
MY NAME

'I didn't ask you to come every day,' I moaned, hating myself the second the words were out of my mouth. My mum and Nan looked down at me with a mixture of confusion and hurt. 'Well, fine by us,' snapped Mum. 'We won't bother to come again then.'

As I watched Mum and Nan leave the ward, I felt more miserable and more alone than I'd ever felt in my whole life. I was facing a life-saving, and potentially life-threatening, operation and I'd just pushed away two of the people closest to me.

Just after returning to Bradford from the Houdini celebrations in New York, my Crohn's worsened. I had been managing it with limited success; I was often very sick and would struggle to get through even a week without some kind of complication. I was constantly in pain and always felt weak.

It got so bad; the pain was so severe that one day I simply couldn't get out of bed. I lay there, unable to move, trying to deal with the pain that no amount of painkillers seemed able to control. My mum took one look at me and left the room straightaway. 'I'm calling an ambulance' she said.

A few minutes later the paramedics arrived. My mum explained my condition and with grave faces they carried me into the ambulance and sped off in the direction of Bradford Royal Infirmary.

It took weeks for the doctors to figure out what was wrong with me. They knew it was my Crohn's, but they couldn't work out what was making it so bad. I lay in bed for days on end in serious pain. They put cameras down, cameras up, gave me barium meals, scans and all sorts of tests and drinks, poking and prodding me relentlessly. Finally, after four and a half months of pretty much staring at a ceiling, I was diagnosed with a stomach abscess.

At first I was relieved; they had pinpointed the problem. But then, as the doctor continued to explain the complexities of my condition, fear started to build. 'You're in a serious situation, Steven,' he said. 'We only really have two options. We can put you on a dialysis machine, which will mean you'll be in hospital for months to come. That is still being tested, though, so we're still unsure how successful the procedure will be. It's a lengthy process and one we're still not sure will even work. The other option we have is major surgery to remove the abscess and a portion of your small bowel.'

I wasn't too keen on the sound of either option, to be honest. To make matters worse, the operation to remove the abcess was potentially very dangerous. 'I have to tell you that the procedure could be life-threatening,' the doctor added. 'There's a large risk that you might not survive. Either way, we have to do one or the other, or face very serious consequences.'

I had an ultimatum: either I went on a dialysis machine or had a life-threatening operation to remove part of my small bowel. If I did neither, I might not have long left to live.

It was, and remains, the most difficult decision I've ever had to make in my life.

With dialysis I would have been in hospital for a lot longer; I would have had to sit in there for months on end hooked up to a drip for something that might not even work. I didn't want to be stuck in the hospital for any more time than was absolutely necessary – there was so much I wanted to do. I'd already been there over four months. Cooped up within the same four walls, after all of my adventures so far, I couldn't face staying there any longer. But if I chose to have the operation, there was a chance I could die.

Rather than discussing the decision with my mum, I rang her now ex-husband, the father of my brothers, Troy and Lee. I needed someone to help me make a practical, rather than emotional decision. My mum would have reached a decision based on what the doctor was saying, but I knew that her ex-husband would be able to offer more reasoned advice that wasn't clouded by maternal instinct. And I needed that. He would help me to decide what was best for me.

After three sleepless and fraught nights, I decided to have the operation. I figured that it might be the riskier option, but at least I had a stronger chance of getting better.

I really upset my mum by not consulting her first. She and my nan had been coming every day for the last four months. It must have so hard for them, especially when I'd be so grouchy when they turned up.

Being in hospital for so long was pretty terrible. The only upsides of the day were watching certain television programmes that always happened to be on at the same time as visiting hours. So, I'd get frustrated. I didn't mean to, I was just depressed. My nan would come every day at five o'clock and I wouldn't be able to watch the TV show I'd wanted to see. 'What did you do today?' she'd ask, day in, day out. I'd rack my brain to think of something new to say. 'They let me have ice cream,' I'd mumble.

It just became mundane. How much can you talk about what you've eaten? What is there to say about how green the walls are? Not only was I very young to be spending so long in hospital, but everyone in my ward was old. My friends were out in the real world having fun, and I was stuck in a room with seriously ill and dying old men, who were coughing and moaning all the time. It was depressing.

I was incredibly grateful to have visitors, but I have to say I was sometimes pretty grumpy! The day before my operation, I was particularly moody. I was on edge, knowing that I might not wake up the next day.

'Cheer up, we came to see you,' my mum said.

'Yeah, but I didn't ask you to come today,' I sighed. 'You're choosing to come here, I'm not choosing to be in here.'

I was frustrated and feeling rather guilty after Mum had also brought up the fact that I hadn't spoken to her about my decision to have the operation. Her eyes were a clouded with fear, anger, sadness. I felt so bad. After our heated exchange, Mum and Nan left and I was left alone.

That night, I somehow managed to sleep and when I woke up the next morning, the anaesthetist arrived to give me my injection. Neither Mum nor Nan was there.

As I slipped into unconsciousness I regretted the stupid argument with my family. They were just trying to be there for me; I had pushed them away.

Hours later, I came to in a huge amount of pain. I opened my eyes and my mum was by my side. 'Sorry, love,' she said. I tried a smile. 'I'm sorry too,' I croaked.

I must have fallen asleep again, because when I woke up it was later in the evening and my mum had gone. My entire body ached. It took me a minute to notice, but my legs felt strange. I went to move them and nothing happened. Panic began to rise in my chest and I struggled for air; I couldn't move my legs. Everything just felt warm. I tried to move my head to see if I could see a nurse, but I had so little energy I couldn't even push the emergency call button. The amount of painkillers I had been given meant I was unable to keep my eyes open. And, before I knew it, I'd sunk back into a deep sleep.

It was the following morning when I finally came around. Once more, Mum was by my side, holding my hand, and the doctor was standing beside her, with my charts. 'How are you feeling today, Steven?' he asked, peering over his clipboard. 'OK', I said, before I remembered. Once more, I tried to move my legs, but nothing happened, there was just a weird, warm sensation.

'My legs,' I gasped. I was so dehydrated that the doctor and my mum could barely hear what I was saying. He explained that they had had to work around my nervous system in order to remove part of my bowel. It meant that I would have temporary paralysis in my legs, but he assured me the feeling would return although I would need to train myself to walk again. My mum looked like she was about to burst into tears. I wasn't feeling much better either.

Just a few months earlier, I'd been hotly pursuing a dream to become a magician, gallivanting all over the world. Now, I was bedbound and worried I may never be able to walk again. Resentment growled inside me as my dreams came crashing

down around me. I felt far from a 'dynamo' now. I felt like giving up all together.

A few days after the operation, the doctor came back to see me. 'We removed part of the bowel,' he explained. 'We cut out the bit that's bad and tied a little bit together in the middle, so you've got a bit of bowel now that's all good…well, for a few years, until it gets bad again…' His voice was becoming increasingly quiet, until suddenly he picked up again. 'Do you feel better? Do you feel normal now?' he asked.

The question stopped me in my tracks. I hadn't felt normal for the first twenty years of my life, so I wasn't sure what he meant. *'You have just cut half my tummy out. Yeah, I guess I feel normal…is this normal?'* I don't know that I've ever felt normal. What is normal?

♠

The next six weeks were the longest of my life. Thankfully, the feeling in my legs slowly returned, but I had to learn to walk all over again. It was so frustrating, taking baby steps, almost falling over like an old man along the way. It's something I never want to have to go through again.

I had to keep reminding myself of the most important thing, that I'd made it through. I was still alive. I was incredibly lucky.

The one upside to being in hospital was that I had ample opportunity to catch up on the latest film releases. Andy, from the video store where I used to work, brought me in a couple of films to watch on the hospital's cranky old VHS player. One day, I was lying on thickly starched sheets, staring blankly at the green walls, fiddling with my cards, and half-heartedly watching the film *Troy*, starring Brad Pitt.

There's a bit in the film where a little kid goes up to Brad Pitt's character, Achilles, and says of the Thessalonian who Achilles was about to fight: 'He's the biggest man I've ever seen. I wouldn't want to fight him.' Pitt turns to the boy and replies, 'That's why no one will remember your name.'

Now, I wasn't harbouring ideas to become a crazed hard-nut ready to take on the biggest guys in Bradford. But that line suddenly and inexplicably struck me. If I died, who would remember my name? What memorable things had I done in my life? I felt goose bumps prickle my skin.

I could have died a few days before and it struck me that, if the worst had happened, that would be it. I'd have my friends and family at my funeral, but who else would care? What mark had I made on the world?

Inside, I could feel the clouds of depression dispersing inside me. It was like a revelation was taking place.

Although I'd been heavily involved in magic, meeting other magicians, travelling to America to trade shows and conferences, and building my name in the UK, I was really still an amateur. I was good at magic, but I was far from great.

I'd seen the way that magic could unite people when I was bullied as a kid. Regardless of race, ethnicity, class or background. Even the ones that used to pick on me suddenly wanted to be my best friend. Imagine if I could spread that feeling around the world?

I had the potential to change things, to bring happiness to people's lives, if only for a few minutes at a time.

Suddenly, a fierce determination roared inside me. I could either languish in this hospital bed, or I could use this opportunity to do something. Something big.

I knew, there and then, that I had to make my mark before it was too late. Having nearly died impressed upon me the importance of seizing each day. It gave me the chance to re-evaluate what I wanted to do. I needed to set up a real business, because until that point I hadn't been running things properly. I'd get bits of cash here, there and everywhere, take random bookings and drive round to clubs with my boys, my little group of loyal friends. I'd made some budget DVDs of which I'd sold maybe a hundred copies, but that wasn't the right way to go about it. There was no structure, no plan. *How can I make it bigger? How can I touch the whole world?*

I needed to make magic my career. It was time to go all out. No matter what the odds.

♠

O nce I'd had my moment of clarity, I was filled with renewed energy and I started devising a plan from my hospital bed, scrawling ideas across bits of paper. I had heard through my old youth club, MAPA, that The Prince's Trust gave out start-up loans for young entrepreneurs who needed a helping hand.

What would I need to do to impress The Prince's Trust to give me the money I needed to get started? I realised I had to have a business plan that would help me stand out from all of the other theatre companies, new businesses and lone entrepreneurs. What could I, Steven Frayne, do that hadn't been done before?

From that moment on, I stopped lying about, watching films and eating grapes. When I wasn't re-learning how to walk and practising my card shuffle, I was thinking about, and writing, my business plan.

At that time, a lot of rappers were becoming famous from self-made mixtapes. The mixtape was a way for a new artist to get

their music out to people without worrying about a record label or a release schedule. You made your music, pressed a few thousand copies and sold them on the streets for a fiver. You had kids everywhere, from Bradford to the Bronx, selling their CD on the streets for a few quid. I loved the DIY mentality, the idea of hustling and not waiting around for anyone.

I'd already dabbled with making CD-ROMs, but now I figured if I was to be taken seriously, I needed something slicker that would make people take no. I needed to emulate this mixtape idea and make a DVD to act, essentially, as my business card.

'You still scribbling that nonsense', the nurses would chuckle as they came to do their rounds. I'd gone into Bradford Royal Infirmary a quiet, worried and, occasionally grumpy, teenager. But something had changed. I was now driven, determined and full of life. It sounds cheesy but I felt like a new person.

I let everything float around in my mind – the line from *Troy*, the way rappers were creating their own hype, and, of course, magic. It was like the perfect storm. I saw that if I fused all of these ideas, incorporating my love of film and music, and focusing on being a magician that was relevant to today, then I might actually be on to something. Using the cultural references of my generation – everything from the films we watched, the music we listened to, to the clothes we wore – I could be my generation's first credible magician.

I devised the idea of a 'Magic Mixtape'; instead of music, it would be a collection of my magic set to the music me and my mates were into. I would need a camera, a laptop and a DVD burner and I'd be good to go. Dynamo's *Underground Magic* would feature me, performing magic on members of the public and the latest, hottest music artists. Combining magic with music, this would be my way of standing out from the rest. No one had ever tried to do anything like this before. All I had to do now was persuade someone to show some financial support.

After six months, I was discharged from hospital. I was weak, and still very sick, but I was determined. I returned to my nan's house and immediately set to work – despite her worrying. 'Stay in bed, you need your rest,' she'd fret. But there was no telling me.

I had fire in my belly and no time to waste.

First of all, I approached the guys at MAPA. It was run by a bloke called Emil, who had seen my work and was hugely supportive of my ambition. Emil introduced me to someone called Tony from one of The Prince's Trust branches in Bradford. 'What do you want to do with your magic?' Tony asked me. I replied confidently: 'I have a business plan. I've got it all sorted out.'

In reality, my 'business plan' consisted of two scrappy pages of A4 and a few half-baked ideas about persuading people to give me a TV show. 'OK, go away and have a proper think about this. The Prince's Trust will need a full, detailed plan. Let's meet next week,' Tony suggested. We started having weekly get togethers to try to help me formulate a proper proposal. Eventually he put me in touch with a business mentor on a regular basis.

To get funding, I went into a meeting where I had to both perform and sell a business idea – it was a bit like *Dragon's Den* crossed with *The X Factor*. I knew my goal was to get enough money to buy the camcorder, laptop, and DVD-burning facilities that I would need to make the first magic mixtape. But first I had to persuade the representatives from The Prince's Trust, who held the keys to the funding.

I walked into the small meeting room at the Providence Insurances office, who were partners with The Prince's Trust in

Bradford at that time. It was everything you'd imagine from an insurance office: bright fluorescent lighting, brown carpet and turgid green walls. There were four guys sitting in a row behind a desk. They were smiling and I could see they were willing me to do well, but it was quite an intimidating environment.

There was no time for nerves – this was my chance to get on the first rung of the ladder in my career. I had nothing to lose. I'd just come out of hospital and nearly died. Normally I might have been intimidated by a situation like this, but I had a new-found confidence; I was fired up and determined to blow them away.

I went in and performed for about twelve minutes. I did the Paul and Ben strength piece; I 'broke' my finger in front of them and then fixed it again before flipping and shuffling my cards, making them appear here, there and everywhere. When I eventually walked out of the room I left them in a state of shock. Five minutes later, one of the guys came out. 'We don't normally do this,' he said. 'Ordinarily you get a letter in the post, but we want to tell you that you've got the funding.' I was completely and utterly taken aback. I'd done it. My plan had worked. I'd explained to them how the likes of 50 Cent had started out by making mixtapes and I wanted to do the same thing, but with magic. The guy continued, 'To be honest, we don't entirely understand what your business is about, but your talent and passion are obvious. We're going to support you in any way we can.'

They gave me £2,000. I'd made it happen. I had my own business. I rushed out to buy a laptop and camera and set to work on my DVD mixtape: *Underground Magic*.

♠

I t was thanks to promoters like Drum Major and Original Heroes that I was able to start meeting a lot of artists, some of whom would later end up on the DVD. Those guys used to promote all the nights in Leeds and Sheffield, and they gave me a lot of bookings for Leeds University.

They also had a lot of connections with the hip-hop world. Through them, I met people like Jazzy Jeff, Ms Dynamite, Sway, Roots Manuva, and so on, when they were up north on college tours. They really helped me in the very early days. Thanks to Ms Dynamite and others, I was able to put together a little scrappy leaflet, featuring quotes and pictures of me with her, Sway and so on. It wasn't much, but it was a start.

Original Heroes ended up doing the Leeds night for the DVD release of Eminem's film, *8 Mile*. It was an *8 Mile* MC Championship and it featured some of the hottest freestylers from Leeds battling each other to win a place in the London finals. I blagged my way into the VIP area, got out my cards and started doing some magic. This guy walks up to me. 'So how come you're performing here?' he asked.

'Oh, I was booked by the organiser,' I replied breezily.

'That's funny,' he laughed, 'because *I* am the organiser and I don't remember booking you!'

His name was Dan Albion, but rather than being annoyed with me, he liked the fact I had some balls. I showed him the leaflet I'd put together and he was impressed by that too. Like me, he had had to hustle his way through the industry.

Dan and I stayed in touch and he started to get me a few gigs here and there. Eventually, he told me that he wanted to manage me, but I was a bit reluctant at first. I liked managing myself and I was convinced I needed to be in control of my own destiny. But then he got me a £13,000 booking, doing a tour for Tizer, which was more money than I had ever earned in one go. Dan also had a background in television production and he had a few ideas about how I could approach the making of *Underground Magic*. I had the magic knowledge, Dan knew how we could produce, promote, distribute and market it. I had a great idea and a vision, Dan had the expertise. He knew how to do what I wanted to achieve. The more I learned about him, the more it made sense.

We've worked together ever since. By combining our strengths, we created a killer team. We were like the X-Men!

Shortly after that, I moved down to London and we began shooting *Underground Magic*. We filmed in Walthamstow, popped up to Birmingham and hustled our way backstage at gigs. We understood that we needed a mixture of footage that would feature people in the street, so the ordinary man, woman or kid could connect, as well as popular people already in the limelight to add even more appeal. We knew the power of 'celebrity' would help to make my magic credible. Reaction in magic is everything; without the spectator, magic is nothing.

It was thanks to a friend of ours, Kemi, who used to work for Dan, that we were able to meet major musicians like Snoop Dogg. Kemi had worked with one of the UK's biggest live promoters and she would hook up me and Dan with tickets. After that, it would be up to us to get ourselves backstage and in front of the band.

Once I got myself into the venue, I'd just have to use my skills to blag us backstage. It was hard work persuading people. It was never as straightforward as showing a security guard a card trick and walking through. There were no Jedi mind tricks at work. It was a mixture of northern charm, magic, a certain sense of

The legendary Paul Daniels. I want to do for my generation what he did for his.

I want to leave a
legacy like my heroes

Performing for Holly Valance and friends.

Me and Ian Brown checking out his latest kicks.

On tour with the Kings of Leon.

Hanging with Snoop.

At Cipriani's restaurant with Sam and Richard Branson.

Rihanna in shock!

Chewie and me.

Will Smith and his beautiful family loved my magic.

Tinie Tempah and me backstage.

Pool party in LA. Keeping the crowds entertained.

people seem to love mag

Sharing that magic feeling with another spectator.

I'll never tire of the spectator's reaction.

o matter who they are

At an F1 party with Christian Horner and Bernie Ecclestone.

The best magic duo to ever exist – Penn & Teller.

real magic
comes
from the hear

fearlessness and the willingness to stand outside in the freezing cold for hours on end, waiting for a friend to send out a friend of a friend with one of their friend's spare backstage wristbands.

Eventually we got strategic about it. We worked out who the right people were to impress but even then they wouldn't always go for it. Would we pull this off or would we be kicked out? It was 50/50 at every gig we went to. Sometimes it worked, sometimes it didn't.

The first time I met Snoop, we managed to get ourselves into one backstage area at Wembley Arena, but then they cleared everyone out for some reason. All of these huge security guys just appeared and started showing everyone the exit. 'All right everyone, thanks very much, but it's home time now.'

Dan nudged me and we dropped behind the crowd of people reluctantly leaving and slipped through a side door. It turned out to be the dressing room of support act M.V.P.. I started doing some magic for the band and, as I did, a girl came in.

'Snoop's ready to meet you now,' she said to the band. They turned and started to walk out of the door. Me and Dan caught each other's eye and, knowing what the other was thinking, we cheekily joined the line and followed the band. Before we knew it we were behind the red rope of Snoop's exclusive area of the venue. It was like nothing else I'd ever seen – he had actual palm trees in there and it was absolutely filled with smoke. After they'd been introduced, the lead singer of the support band said to Snoop, 'You have to see what this guy can do'. Snoop looked over at me. 'Oh yeah, what's that then?' he smiled.

I wasn't sure how long I would be able to hold his attention for, so I did something very simple – I made a coin appear underneath his watch. He smiled, turned to his laptop, picked a beat and began to freestyle a rap about me. Dan got the camera

before we knew it we were behind the red rope of Snoop's exclusive area

out, smiling the whole time as Snoop rapped about me. It was so surreal.

Dan and I were over the moon. We had our first bit of footage and it was so much more than we could have ever hoped for. We must have checked back about eight times to make sure we'd recorded it, totally paranoid that Dan had forgotten to press 'record'. It was one of the first times I'd been filmed with a celebrity and that footage turned out to be priceless. We used it everywhere from *Underground Magic* to my showreel. It was the catalyst I'd been looking for.

♠

Blagging soon became second nature. When I first blagged my way backstage at a Coldplay concert, I knew it would be very tough to get Chris Martin's attention. He'd just come offstage and was hanging out with his family and friends. Why would he want to be entertained by someone he'd never met? How could I get to him? I had a video camera with me and I knew this could be a great opportunity to get some incredible footage. I just had to work out how to get myself in front of Chris.

Once again, Kemi had hooked us up with tickets to the show as well as some kind of backstage access, though it was nowhere near the dressing rooms. This meant we would have to do a lot of work to break away from the gathered fans, hangers-on and industry people to get to where the real action was.

We tried to take what we thought was a pretty nonchalant stroll through the warren of the backstage corridors, hoping that no one would spot us and say, 'Oi, what the hell are you two up to?'

As I had suspected, Dan and I couldn't get anywhere near Chris or the band; there was no way the security were going to let us into their inner sanctum. By chance, we saw an older woman in another room down the corridor from the band's dressing room. I wandered in there, said 'Hello' and showed her some card magic. The woman's jaw dropped. 'Chris,' she shouted, 'you have to see this.' Before I knew it, I was being marched down the corridor into the dressing room, with this woman waving her AAA pass at the security.

'Hang on a minute,' said Chris, engrossed in a conversation with his band mates and wife, Gwyneth Paltrow.

'Chris, you really need to see what this magician does,' she urged. Again, he gently batted her away. 'Give me a second, Mum, I'm in the middle of something.'

The woman turned out to be Chris Martin's mum! I'd had no idea at all. His mum all but dragged me under his nose, insisting that Chris check out my magic. Chance had favoured me once again. Eventually, Chris turned his attention towards me. I knew that I had about a five-second window before he'd lose interest, so I performed one quick card levitation and went to leave. But Chris was suddenly on his feet. 'Wait, wait,' he insisted, 'that was

amazing, you have to show the band!' Within seconds, I was surrounded by the whole of Coldplay and Gwyneth. I had a very impressed Chris Martin smiling down at me. 'F*** me, this kid's good,' he grinned.

My heart swelled. We had another piece of killer footage for *Underground Magic*. Thanks Chris's mum!

♠

Showing Snoop and Chris my magic taught me to never give up on a situation – no matter how impossible it might appear. You have to watch for the random opportunities and take them – you don't know who that woman in a small room away from the main action may turn out to be! The door you open might lead to a friendly support act, willing to help out. It might also bring you to the head of security and before you know it, you're out on your ear. But hey, you win some, you lose some.

I think the fact that I can do magic certainly puts me at an advantage. Entertainers perform all over the world and by the time they're famous they've seen it all. It's probably very rare that they witness something that genuinely amazes them. Magic is still only really practised by comparatively few people. If everyone did, it wouldn't be magic. There are lots of rappers, footballers, singers, actors, but you can only really count on two hands the names of magicians who dominate their field. When I meet a rapper or singer, they are usually pleasantly surprised that I'm not another kid trying to get a record deal. I'm just there to perform for them, surprise them, and offer a different perspective on their day. Even for the most jaded of performers, magic can be reinvigorating. They don't know what I'm going to do, and so they're even more amazed when I perform some magic and absolutely smash it.

It's funny that, over the years, I've always managed to get introduced to people, but on the whole it all happens very naturally. A lot of people have commented that – I don't know if this is a weird thing for me to say – I have some sort of magnetism. I think that it's because I've never been someone to want something from other people. I go and perform, but I don't expect anything in return. I've always just wanted to share my gift.

I suppose being a cheeky so-and-so with a fair bit of northern charm, wit and humour doesn't hurt much either. My nan always said I had a sunny disposition. I've always had that little bit of cheekiness about me because I had to, otherwise I'd have been done for on the estate. I definitely picked up the entrepreneurial side from Gramps and possibly my dad. Plus, most of the people I saw around the estate were always hustling a little bit. That spirit of making things happen for yourself has surrounded me for as long as I can remember.

♠

Looking back, it feels like quite a journey from being in hospital to making *Underground Magic*. It was the beginning of my success as a magician: I was featured on the cover of *The Guardian Guide*, *The Sun* wrote a feature on me, and, not long after, Channel 4 approached me to make a one-off special, *Dynamo's Estate of Mind*, while MTV soon followed suit with *Barrio 19* – a programme that showcased street talents around the world.

I honestly don't know how things would have worked out if I hadn't had that serious operation. It really was a life-changing moment. Maybe I'd still be doing magic, maybe I wouldn't. But I do know for certain that being in the hospital filled me with a desire to achieve that hadn't been there before. I had always been driven, but after hospital I had never been more determined, more focused.

My Crohn's is a lot more manageable now. I might be in pain every day, but I hardly ever get hospitalised. I used to be in hospital every few weeks, but I haven't had a flare-up for a couple of years at least. My last downfall was a bag of popcorn at my local cinema. I woke up the next day in devastating pain. Dan rang an ambulance and I was in hospital for two weeks. Since then, touch wood, I haven't had to go back.

When I'm performing, adrenalin kicks in and masks any pain. The magic takes it away and I forget everything: the pain, discomfort, my worries and troubles. Magic literally makes everything vanish.

In some ways, I feel weirdly thankful for my Crohn's – it gave me the jolt-start I needed. Given the choice, of course, I'd rather not have it, as I'd love to be able to lead a normal, pain-free life. But dealing with it has given me inner strength and I have never let it hold me back. It gave me the focus to realise that I could do anything I set my mind to. Anything.

CHAPTER 7

OUT OF THE REALM OF NORMALITY

As I straightened my tie, I took a good, long, hard look in the mirror. Staring back at me was a twenty-one-year-old guy with total disbelief in my eyes. *'How did this happen?'* I thought to myself. It was 2005 and all the effort I'd put into making my *Underground Magic* DVD had paid off. We had pressed 5,000 copies and within a few weeks each and every one had been sold. Dan got all of his mates to help us pack and post them.

Now, in recognition of my success, I'd been invited to a Prince's Trust event at Clarence House – the Prince of Wales' official residence. I was going to meet royalty – Prince Charles – in the flesh. It was unbelievable. Getting ready in the tiny flat in Walthamstow, north-east London, that I was now paying £50 a week to share, I reflected on how life might have been if I'd been born into royalty rather than on an estate.

Ever since I received the loan from The Prince's Trust, I've been heavily involved with a lot of the events they organise. But my first visit to Clarence House, which is where many of the functions are held, will always be my most memorable. When you are invited to Clarence House to meet Prince Charles, you are scrupulously checked over beforehand. At the entrance, you are given a thorough search by big burly guards before you can enter the grounds, then once you're finally in you get whisked straight to the library.

Built in the early nineteenth century, Clarence House is awe-inspiring. The exterior is all towering pillars and imposing wrought-iron gates. Inside, there are sweeping staircases, a library heaving with books and priceless artworks on the perfectly wallpapered walls. Now that I've been more than once, I take the opportunity to notice the finer details. A couple of years ago, Kevin Spacey showed me the first-edition of Shakespeare's *Richard III*, while original paintings by British masters like Graham Sutherland and Augustus John are displayed on the walls. The tea is, needless to say, served in the best china.

It's like going to a museum. I've visited Clarence House twice now and I still feel the thrill of exploring such a different

environment. But that first time was particularly strange. It was so odd to see all these people socialising in such a formal place – they were drinking, laughing and chatting, and seemed so confident and relaxed. But, Dan and I felt really out of place and quite awkward. This world seemed as familiar to me as life on Mars. My tie was tight around my neck and my suit felt suffocating.

But in some ways, if I didn't have the background I have, I don't think I would have appreciated the experience as much as I did. Knowing where I'd come from, and what I'd had to do to get that invitation, made the day even more special. There was little opportunity in Delph Hill. I could have ended up doing nothing with my life, yet here I was, an invited guest at Clarence House.

The best thing about going to a Prince's Trust event is that you have all of these successful and inspirational people, who are being recognised for their achievements, around you. I'm always interested in meeting new people who have had interesting lives. At Clarence House, you see charity directors, film-makers, musicians, designers, photographers, business people, entrepreneurs and actors. All types of people doing all sorts of things from all walks of life. The first time I went Brian May from Queen was there and, for some reason, when I looked across the room and saw him I was weirdly star-struck.

After milling about for a short while, we were then separated into small groups. After a brief wait, there was a hush as Prince Charles and Camilla made their entrance. They were brought in by an assistant, who then took them around the room and formally introduced them to everyone. I watched as each person had a brief conversation with the royal couple, shook their hands and then they'd move on. They had a lot of people to meet, so you only had a small window of time with the Prince and his wife.

As I anxiously awaited my turn, I realised I had to go to the toilet. Excusing myself, I sped off to the facilities at double speed, not wanting to miss my slot with Charles and Camilla. Thankfully, the toilet was close to the library so I didn't have too far to go. Afterwards, I found myself wondering if I'd shared the same throne as the Queen!

I got back just in the nick of time – they were talking to the person next in line to me. As they began to move on, nerves rumbled in my belly. This was it, my moment to show Prince Charles how The Trust's investment had paid off.

The Prince's aide introduced us to each other. 'Your Royal Highness,' I smiled shyly, taking a little bow. There are very proper rules for meeting royalty. When speaking to Prince Charles, you're supposed to refer to him as 'Your Royal Highness' at first, and then 'Sir'.

We had a chat about where I was from and my background, and from then on I let my magic do the talking.

I asked him to think of a card and once he'd chosen one, I held out the deck in front of me. Slowly, one card began to rise out of the deck until it hung in mid-air. It was Prince Charles's card.

'That's wonderful,' Charles laughed as Camilla looked on in amazement.

Not wanting to take up too much of their time, I took another bow so that the next person could have their time with the royal couple.

After they'd moved on, I breathed a sigh of relief and walked off across the room to find myself a glass of water. But then, all of a sudden, I heard a very posh, shrill lady's voice which stopped me in my tracks. 'Young man,' it said. For a second I thought someone was about to accuse me of nicking a vase. However, I spun around only to see Camilla, dragging some kids behind her.

'Wait, wait, you must show these children,' she pleaded. She was so impressed; she had literally chased me across the library so I could perform some magic for her friend's kids. I was well and truly stoked. And the kids loved it.

I've met Prince Charles about six or seven times now, but I don't know what he made of me that first time; I'm not sure they've had anyone doing magic in a royal residence for over a century, and if they have, I don't think they would have looked like me. Obviously, I always put on my best suit when I am invited to Clarence House – imagine what my nan would say if I rolled up in my trainers!

Whenever I see Prince Charles now, he's like, 'How are you doing, Dynamo? How's tricks?' The Prince is actually pretty cool. I don't know if he's given last-minute briefings about the people he is meeting, or if it's just that he's very up to date with popular culture, but he's one of the most well-informed people I've ever met.

Prince Charles doesn't seem to have an agenda. When he asked me a question and I gave him an answer, he really listened to what I was saying. He replied with something that was actually relevant to what I was saying. That really surprised me. He took the time and he made me feel special. As well as telling him where I was from, and how I got into magic. I told him about the bullies and Gramps, and how The Prince's Trust had given me a £2,000 loan to make my first-ever DVD. He didn't have to listen to all of that – he's going to be King at some point; he can do what he wants.

Sometimes he gets a bit of flak, but I think people don't always understand him. And I believe he gives a lot back with the work he does with The Prince's Trust.

Although I haven't met Prince William yet, I was introduced to Prince Harry a couple of years ago at a charity fund-raising dinner for the International Olympic Committee.

I brought my boy Gilera, who's also my driver, and Dennis, who does my dance choreography. Wherever I go, I try to take my friends along so that we can experience these things together and share the adventure. I think I'd told them we were going to some sort of sporting event and they turned up in trainers and do-rags. When we turned up at the dinner, it was black tie; everyone was suited and booted, and it took place at the Grosvenor Hotel in London – a very fancy place. My mates felt really uncomfortable and after I had performed, they sloped off somewhere.

I finished my slot with my infamous lean-back where I'm suspended in mid-air, then I went off to try to find the guys. I started up some stairs to a roped-off balcony area which had been reserved for the people who were performing or talking at the event. Even before I got to the top of the stairs, I could hear all this laughter.

When I got there, I found Dennis and Gilera with Prince Harry, joking around. My boys were teaching him some dance moves and Harry was trying to do the lean-back – without much success!

If I'd had to guess who out of all the people downstairs that Harry would have ended up hanging out with, those two would have been last on my list.

Watching them mucking about, it struck me that, essentially, people are people. Harry was really cool, very normal, just a young guy who liked having a laugh – like we all do. It reminded me that if you can see past all of your own preconceptions, it doesn't matter where someone is from. I love that things like magic, as well as film, literature, music, art, dance, has the incredible ability to transcend class and other divisions in society. It brings people together, people who might ordinarily never have got to meet each other.

♠

I went back to Clarence House in 2011 for the thirty-fifth birthday of The Prince's Trust. There was everyone from Rod Stewart to the Bond girl Gemma Arterton and the actor Dominic West from *The Wire*. Once again, we were split into different groups – I was with Kevin Spacey – and I knew I had that small window to really blow Prince Charles away.

I asked the Prince if he was a gambling man, and then I took out some lottery tickets. With a quick shake, I instantly changed them into a stack of crisp £50 notes. Everyone gasped and Charles chuckled. With that, my time was done but I think I'd impressed him. Charles said he'd like to take me home to perform for his mum. That would be my pleasure, Your Majesty!

My experiences at Clarence House put things in some sort of perspective and allowed me to give myself a small pat on the back. Although the first time I went, I probably thought that I was close to making it, in reality I was years away. But on that first visit, with Camilla chasing me about, and Brian May watching me do my magic, I felt quite proud of how far I'd come. I was trying to create something out of nothing and I didn't let rejection stand in my way. In the years following, I had to face a lot of disappointments and knock-backs – and I'm sure there are more of those to come. But getting myself in that door with royalty was a real vindication of my early ambition.

I'm incredibly grateful to The Prince's Trust. I might not be writing this book right now if it weren't for them. I'm very thankful for the £2,000 start-up loan that they gave me because it enabled me to buy the equipment I needed, but also it let me know that someone had faith in me. The Trust helped me to see that you can achieve things out of the realm of normality.

♠

From Prince Charles to the Fresh Prince of Bel-Air… It was through The Prince's Trust that, two years after my first visit to Clarence House, I got to meet one of my heroes.

It was 2007 and The Prince's Trust was holding a lunch at the Dorchester Hotel for their Celebrate Success Awards. That year they combined it with the premiere of Will Smith's film, *The Pursuit of Happyness*. I was there to be recognised as someone who had achieved success through The Prince's Trust.

The event was held in one of the hotel's ballrooms and there were well over a hundred esteemed guests from the film and charity industries. Because I felt uncomfortable dressing up, I wore my baseball cap and trainers; everyone else looked incredibly smart. I felt a bit out of place, but by then I was growing in confidence.

Before the awards ceremony started, me and a few others who had been helped by The Prince's Trust were asked to set up a display of our work in a room behind the main hall. Dan and I had arrived early to get ready. I had my *Underground Magic* DVD cover, a laptop playing the DVD and my cards all set up on a little table in the corner. Prince Charles was brought around and, as always, he remembered me straight away. We had a brief chat and then, about five minutes later, Will Smith came by with his wife Jada and his kids, Jaden and Willow.

As soon as Will walked into the room, everyone stopped talking. He's a pretty magnetic guy. He's also incredibly polite and down to earth, and, like Prince Charles, actually listens to what you say.

I reminded Will that I had met him briefly three years ago at The Prince's Trust Urban Music Festival. He said he remembered me, but I'm not sure if he did! We'd performed something for him and Dan had tried, unsuccessfully, to get a picture of us together. The camera wouldn't work and, eventually, Will had to leave.

He laughed when I reminded him, and I did a load of magic for him and his kids; his son Jaden all but ran away when I broke my finger in two and Willow seemed pretty freaked out when I pushed a coin through the bottom of a Coke bottle.

Will and his family were really gracious and as we shook hands he said, 'Magical. Truly magical.'

After my presentation, I wasn't supposed to be doing any more magic. They said that I would be brought up onstage and given my award by the actress Thandie Newton and we'd have a brief interview about the highs and lows of my life and career.

As I waited in the candlelit ballroom, distractedly picking at the food that had been laid on, Dan leant over and said, 'I think you should have something ready to do onstage.' I looked at his mischievous grin. 'Really?' I asked, unsure. It was a very formal environment and I didn't want to upset the balance of things or break some weird protocol. 'Definitely,' he said. 'We're in a room with some of the biggest players in the film industry; let's have something ready and if it feels right when you get up onstage, you should definitely do it. You only get one shot in life at things like this; take it. Magic is what you do; get up there and do it.'

Joanna Lumley was the host and she introduced the gorgeous Thandie Newton. Thandie asked me to come to the stage, where she started to conduct an interview with me.

'You obviously have a brilliant talent, and you bring so much enjoyment to people. But you had a difficult time growing up; can you share with us a little bit about the beginnings of your career...?'

As she spoke, Dan's voice echoed inside my head. *Get up there and do it.* I looked across at Thandie.

'Sorry, my nan always said I should have fresh breath,' I said, cutting her off. I took out a Polo mint, swallowed it, and offered her one. 'A gentleman as well,' she noted, before nodding at me to encourage me to tell my story. Suddenly, I started choking. Thandie looked panicked and when I clutched my neck and slowly pulled the Polo mint through my skin and out of my throat on a chain, her face drained of blood. Everyone else in the room gasped in a mixture of shock and horror and I could hear Will Smith in the audience, laughing heartily. Thandie tried to steer the interview back on course, but I had totally thrown her. It was a fairly naughty stunt I had pulled on her. Eventually she wrapped things up and presented me with an award that was signed by Will Smith.

Feeling pretty pleased with myself, I jumped offstage as Will got up to do a speech about his film. But before he got on with promoting his film, he appeared to divert from his pre-prepared speech.

'Listen, I know we've moved on, but that man just pulled a Life Saver [polo mint] out of his neck,' he grinned, looking over at me. 'That is absolutely stunning. You scared my son with your tricks earlier – but magic just gets me like that. When I think about being able to take something that doesn't exist right now and create it out of thin air... it really is magic. The idea of life and living and being able to sit in your home... and you see a picture of who you want to be, and none of it exists right now. The journey that you have to take to achieve it, that is magic to me.'

This was one of the best speeches I've ever heard about magic and something I'll never forget. If magic is indeed creating something out of nothing, then magic is everywhere.

If you think about it, just about everything in our lives is created from human thought. And that's magical. The internet, the wheel, incredible architecture and design, books, films... It's all magic. It all started out as a thought in someone's head and by magic it materialised.

Those words that Will said that day have stayed with me ever since. Whenever it got tough over the following few years, I recalled Will's speech. I couldn't give up on magic; it was my responsibility to keep going. To keep the magic alive.

♠

For me, magic isn't about 'fooling' people, it's about sharing that sense of wonder and excitement and amazement. It's about creating a moment of awe where, for a short time, anything is possible. Magic isn't about 'tricking'

people or making them feel stupid; it's about opening the realms of possibility and creating a moment of joy.

I don't do 'tricks'. I perform magic. I remember hearing some wise words from my friend Maseo, who is part of the legendary trio, De La Soul.

A few years ago, Maseo asked me to perform at his kid's birthday party, because his children are huge fans of mine. In return, he offered to pay for mine and Dan's flights to Miami, put us up and show us all of the sights.

He took us on a crazy tour of Miami. We went everywhere from the infamous Ocean Drive to Downtown before we stopped off in a place called Boca Raton, which is where all of the retired mafia hang out. It's a place with a real edge to it and you meet some very interesting characters there. We stopped by a tattoo parlour and I did some magic.

Afterwards, we went to a Denny's, which is a fast-food chain in the US. As me, Dan and Maseo left, an old guy who had been hanging around the tattoo parlour approached us.

'Hey, kid, do some more tricks,' he asked.

Maseo shook his head. 'It's not tricks, man, it's magic,' he said, before turning to me and Dan. 'People hate tricks because they think they're being fooled. What you do is amazing, and magic is about amazing people, not tricking them or making them look foolish.'

It was another very important moment in my journey because Maseo really impressed upon me the importance of the terminology I used and also the way that I wanted people to think about magic. Magic is not about demeaning people; it's about inspiring people.

I do feel a responsibility not to let people down. They want to experience magic, to feel that wonder of not being able to understand something. I guess it's the only time people are taken back to their childhood, when everything in life was completely amazing and fun. Similarly, I don't use the word 'fans' either, because I think that too implies that you're somehow 'above' people. My magic is about uniting everyone, not putting myself on a pedestal.

There's a good reason for that too. The thing I missed most as a kid was a family life. I had my mum and grandparents, but it wasn't a 'Mum and Dad' family like my friends had. I always longed for that security. Magic was my way of bringing people together, and now I feel like my Twitter followers, who have named themselves the '#Dynamites', are all a part of that community.

I'm not a leader – I'm just one guy. But I do want to inspire people and I think that I can inspire people. I owe it to everyone else and I owe it to all the people who have helped me along the way. I couldn't have got this far on my own. I may have performed the magic, but everyone from my manager Dan, to The Prince's Trust, to Will Smith, to the promoters who booked me and the newspapers that helped me tell my story, have all played a part. It was my duty to share the gift I have, but I'm acutely aware that without help along the way, I wouldn't have been able to reach people in the way that I have.

You should never forget that one person alone achieves very little.

CHAPTER 8

WHO'S THE MAGICIAN?

As my career began to take off, exploring new weird and wonderful places became a more regular thing for me. In my time, I've found myself in the most amazing places and my journey has been full of surprises. Sometimes the unexpected and the unplanned can be one of life's greatest gifts.

In terms of some of the places I've ended up, Singapore has to be among the most outrageous. I have a few friends who live out there and it's always a bit ridiculous; when we go out, we roll in a convoy of Ferraris, drop-top Phantoms and Porsches – the most over-the-top cars you've seen. It's like something from the Gumball Rally. Our friends in Singapore look after us very well – they're internet entrepreneurs and very successful, so it can be crazy seeing life through their eyes. It's the funny thing about my new way of life: one minute I'm at Ronnie Wood's birthday party in his house, the next I'm in the shanty towns of Brazil. Even to this day, I pinch myself. Dan and I will look at each other like, 'How the hell did we end up here?' Some of the hotel suites I've booked into in Dubai or Singapore would fit my entire flat in them twenty times over.

It's in cities like Dubai, Abu Dhabi and Singapore where I've witnessed wealth on an incredible scale. It's thanks to Formula

One that I've been invited to these cities in the first place; and it's through them I've met many of the people I admire such as Richard Branson and Pharrell Williams, and hung out with the likes of Lewis Hamilton.

In December 2009, Formula One invited me to the Singapore Grand Prix to perform for F1 Rocks. An idea was floated around that I would drive Beyoncé around a racing track – blindfolded. Unsurprisingly, perhaps, her team went off the idea of letting their multi-million-selling artist hurtle around a racetrack at 150mph with a blind kid from Bradford behind the wheel.

So we approached someone else instead: Lindsay Lohan. Now, ordinarily I like to have at least a little bit of time to hang out with someone before we film, just so I can get to know them a little. But when you are dealing with a huge celebrity, it is often the problem that they only have a very limited amount of time to spare. It can really put the pressure on when it comes to getting the footage you need.

Lindsay had had a nightmare getting to Singapore, missing four flights and being delayed all around the world as she tried to make her way from LA. As soon as she landed, she was piled into a car, which raced her to a huge shopping mall in the middle of the city.

It was a boiling hot day. The steel-clad building omitted heat all around us; it was touching 40°C at one point and the humidity was off the scale. In order to reach me, Dan had to guide Lindsay through the vast shopping mall, packed with thousands of people. After trawling through the shops, up the back stairs and in and out of various lifts for half an hour, they eventually stumbled up onto the roof. We were supposed to have an hour to get the shot, but we only had twenty minutes by the time she arrived.

It was so hot; I thought we were both going to pass out. We'd had to hire industrial fans to try to keep us cool enough so we didn't sweat our way through the shoot. Time was so tight; we only had one shot, and one shot only, to get it right.

Lindsay perched on top of a bar stool and I asked her to hold my hand as she closed her eyes. By this time a curious crowd had gathered, adding to the tension. I stood back and levitated her off the chair. Slowly, she rose up into the air. But rather than freak out, Lindsay giggled nervously, trying to keep as calm and composed as possible. Up and up she rose, until there was a metre-long gap between her and the chair. I passed my hands beneath her to show there was nothing there.

The gathered audience had a 360-degree view of what was happening. Their mouths opened wide as they stared at Lindsay, in her little vest and skirt, floating in mid-air among all the magnificent buildings in Singapore. It was a real sight.

In the twenty minutes we spent together, we got on really well and I think she enjoyed doing something a little out of the ordinary. I've seen Lindsay since then in Cannes and in London, and she's always really cool.

Singapore was hard work – it just seemed to get hotter and hotter and it took a lot to persuade people to give me even two minutes of their time. I wanted to do a good job for F1 Rocks, as they had flown me out there, so I knew they'd be counting on me to get great footage of the various stars who had also been brought over for Formula One.

Will.i.am was really jet-lagged and overheated. I could tell it would be a challenge to engage him. So I left him alone to chill out and instead showed Taboo from the Black Eyed Peas some magic. I pulled something off that had Taboo, and his band mate Apl, going crazy. I snapped a piece of string off my T-shirt, swallowed it and then I lifted up my T-shirt to reveal my stomach. Protuding from it was the piece of white thread. My skin puckered as I pulled and pulled until the string was free from my body. Their reaction was brilliant – they ran about like headless chickens as they tried to process what they'd just seen. Eventually, Will.i.am burst out laughing and really got involved.

As Will Smith once said, people are attracted to greatness. If you can display greatness in whatever field you work in, then naturally people are going to gravitate towards you. Plant the seed around them and they will come. It's keeping them there that is the hard part.

It's a principle I apply today. Sometimes I need to attract the attention of an A-lister because I've been asked to create content for something, like, for instance, F1 Rocks or the MTV VMA Awards show. So, I'll need to 'work the room' and get footage of the more famous people in the room because that's essentially what I'm there for. The company relies on the bigger names to get viewers to either watch on TV or look online.

I've found when I'm in a room with a celebrity I can inadvertently steal the attention from them. It's not intentional, but the curiosity of the crowd will invariably be drawn towards what I'm doing when I perform. I start small, working the room, so that people slowly get an awareness of what's going on. I've found that occasionally with a famous person, as the hangers-on and pretty girls start to gather around me, their attention and curiosity will override whatever they're doing and ultimately they too will want to see what everybody is so excited about.

It was a lesson I first learnt when I performed for Jay-Z. It was 2006 at the Light Bar in London's Covent Garden. He was throwing a party for the release of his album, *Kingdom Come*. It was your typical West End scene – so dimly lit you could barely

a lot of people
have said that I
have some sort
of magnetism

see the end of your nose, with over-priced cocktails and a long, winding queue outside waiting to get in. That night, the Light Bar was the place to be. 'Hi guys, come on in,' said the hostess, welcoming me and Dan, despite our caps and trainers. My face was fast becoming a familiar sight at bars around the West End. I was far from famous, but I was starting to get a certain amount of recognition. I didn't have to work as hard to blag my way in anymore; they knew I'd do some magic and help everyone have a good time.

Around midnight, the moment everyone had been waiting for finally arrived: Jay-Z made his entrance. Everyone rushed towards him, pushing against the black rope of the VIP area. Wearing dark shades, designer clothes and jewellery, his fame, confidence and talent lit up the room.

We didn't have a camera with us, so I knew I wouldn't be able to create any content. But as an admirer and long-term fan of Jay-Z, I simply wanted to perform for him. I was genuinely interested to find out what he thought of my magic.

Dan and I were probably the only two people in the room who didn't go over and crowd around him. I stood to the side and started messing with my cards. Gradually, people stopped staring at the world-famous rapper and drifted back to their seats. Jay-Z had said a few polite 'hellos' and before long the whole club was jumping. People were up for a party.

I started doing my special card shuffle, nothing too crazy, but enough to gather a circle of people around me. 'Hey bro, do that one where you put the coin in the bottle?' said one enthusiastic bystander. I was starting to generate a lot of attention.

After about five minutes, Jay-Z's best friend, Ty Ty, clocked what was going on. I could feel him watching me for a while before he tapped Jay-Z on the shoulder. The next thing I knew the entire party had descended on me – Jay-Z and his crew had sauntered over.

I did some card magic on Jay-Z and Ty Ty. 'This kid is dope,' they murmured. He might have been a famous rapper but that night Jay-Z was just like anyone else – a curious bystander caught up in the wonder.

I finished with a final big piece of magic – I made his signature magically appear on my business card – and left. *Pow!* That's the best way, I think – leave them wanting more.

The next night, Dan and I were out again in the West End, and we saw Jay-Z and his crew celebrating his birthday at Movida. 'Hey, get over here,' said Jay-Z, beckoning us over to his table that was heaving with both champagne and beautiful women. 'Show me some more of what you got.' Well, it would have been rude not to!

♠

A few years later, I met Lewis Hamilton for the first time. He'd just started to win a lot of races, and we'd both been invited to the 2007 MTV EMA Awards in Munich.

It was well after midnight and people were already pretty tipsy from the awards show. A big brand threw an after-party and so we decided to go to this crazy event in some cavernous warehouse in deepest, darkest Munich to see what was going on. There was a lot of alcohol and the loudest music was blasting from the speakers. It was a real celebrity-filled party. Everyone from the Black Eyed Peas to the Foo Fighters and the Pussycat Dolls were there.

I was out partying with Lewis Hamilton and Shaggy (a random combination to say the least)! I don't remember too much about how the night ended. I just know it was crazy and that a few days later my friend Lewis was dating a Pussycat Doll. Sounds like a good night to me!

I bumped into Lewis again in Singapore two years later. I was with a friend whose father is a big deal in the oil industry and rather wealthy! Life was good as me and my friend's mates drove around the city. I was in a Ferrari while my friend was in a Bentley – both of them matte white. I'm bit of a petrol head and the sight of them gave me palpitations! They were so cool.

At one point we pulled up at some traffic lights. I looked to the left and I could see these guys checking out the car from a taxi. My face lit up as I realised who was in the taxi – it was Lewis! Obviously, Formula One was on and he was in town.

He wound the taxi window down. 'Dynamo! What are you doing here?' he shouted.

I explained I was filming for Formula One and just as we'd established that we were staying at the same hotel, the lights changed. 'You want to race back?' I grinned. To be fair, he wasn't driving and he was in a taxi, but to me it was a race, which I won nonetheless. It was nuts: Lewis Hamilton, a famous Formula One driver, and I beat him in a race.

Since then, I've performed at Lewis's birthday party and we hang out here and there. He became a lot more famous faster than I did, but then again he is a Formula One driver. He's still a really good, genuine guy despite his success.

Magic has introduced me to such a broad range of people. I have my best mates from home who do everything from teaching to working for British Gas; I have friends who I work with and I have pals from all over the world of entertainment, including sports like football, racing and boxing.

David Haye, for instance, has been a great friend. It's a pretty incredible feeling when you get to sit ringside at one of his fights. And he is always happy to join in on my magic. I've had a lot of support from Wayne Rooney and Rio Ferdinand too. I love seeing these big, strong sportsmen running around in amazement like kids because of some magic I've created. It never fails to amuse me – and them.

♠

It was through Formula One that I met Richard Branson for the first time. They had invited me out to Abu Dhabi to perform and then they took me out for dinner while I was out there. We went to a place called Cipriani's. It's a beautiful restaurant.

Dan and I were having dinner when I noticed Sam Branson, Richard's son. I first met Sam through my friend Johnny. I've known Johnny since school. He used to be a professional wakeboarder and would often wakeboard with Sam.

I got to know Sam and his sister Holly through Johnny, and over the years we've hung out together. I've done a lot of work with Sam for his family's charity, Virgin Unite, too.

Sam noticed me at Cipriani's and called me over, saying, 'Dad, this is the magician – Dynamo – I was telling you about. D, would you mind showing my dad some of your magic?' I'd read quite a few of his business books and knew it would be a great opportunity to show someone I admire what I could do.

There was no one filming, there was no one else really watching, so it was quite a low-key, private moment. Usually when I perform it often becomes a case of camera-phones and crowds with everyone craning to see what's going on. It was a special moment between me, Sam, Richard and his friends.

I asked Richard to pull out a coin from his wallet. I made him close his fist over it and the next thing he knew the coin had disappeared from his hand and reappeared under his watch. I then made his watch disappear. It was just spur-of-the-moment fun, totally improvised, but that was what made it good. How magic should be. If I'd known I was going to do magic for Richard Branson that night I might have over-thought what I was going to do, which could have ruined what was such a natural, relaxed moment.

At the end, he got off his chair, dropped to the ground and started bowing down to me. Sir Richard Branson was on the floor, on his hands and knees, his face just inches away from my trainers. That's right, Sir Richard Branson on his knees, bowing to me. It was surreal. Part of me didn't know what to do, though I do remember thinking, '*Oh, I wish someone had a camera right now.*' To my delight, Richard then turned to his son and said, 'Take a picture, Sam, take a picture,' while he stayed there bowing down to me on the floor. Bizarre.

You know when Richard Branson is in the room. There are no airs or graces. Just confidence and a sense of power and presence. I guess that when you've reached the level of success he has, you've probably dealt with a lot of your demons and your insecurities, so you just exude confidence.

He's always smiling. I've met a few super-rich businessmen over the years and a lot of the time you can see the stress of their responsibilities weighing them down. But with Richard he's having a wicked time, no matter what he's doing. I think he wholeheartedly embraces life.

About a year after Cipriani's, Sam booked me to perform at the wedding of his sister, Holly, and her husband, Freddie. I was a 'gift' from Sam.

The reception was at the Kensington Roof Gardens, which is a glamorous private members' club that Richard Branson owns. It was a very lavish do with lots of incredible food and drink laid on for the guests. When I first saw Richard he had crowd of people around him because, naturally, everyone wanted to congratulate him. So, I just walked past and said a quick 'hello'.

Later on, I took my cards, coins and Polo mints (my tools of the trade) from table to table and entertained them all. I didn't feel like there was a pressure; I just went, did my thing and had a great time. The guests reacted so well. Everyone was in great spirits and because it was such a magical day anyway they really embraced my magic too. They wanted to believe to make the day even more special. From Richard, Sam and Holly to their family and friends, I felt really lucky to have been able to add to what was such a special occasion.

That's the thing I love about magic: it doesn't matter if you're a kid from Bradford, a big-shot celebrity, or a billionaire businessman – it puts everyone on the same level. For me, the reactions from people are everything. I love the looks on their faces – sometimes they laugh, sometimes they're shocked, some people even get scared. But there's always that one moment when I look at them and I see a glint in their eye and for that second they believe that anything is possible. I'll never stop loving that moment.

♠

It's only really been in the last year or two that I've come to fully understand why I feel the need to do magic. Like I've said, the way it brings people together is right up there; the way I can bring a moment of astonishment into their lives and show them the impossible, but it's also because I can affect people's lives in other ways.

I get to work with a lot of charities and I'm always amazed by what they do. Where possible, I like to do something to try to help out. And the purity of magic seems to be a good fit, especially for kids' charities.

I've spent a lot of time in hospital myself and I know how depressing and glum it can be. But thanks to groups like the Teenage Cancer Trust and other children's charities, the day-to-day experience for these kids is made slightly more bearable.

When the Euro 2012 tournament was taking place, I decided to put on a bet and predicted the outcome of the final. But I went quite a few steps further. I predicted all of the quarter-final winners – Portugal, Spain, Italy and Germany – and said that Italy would win on penalties. And, that Spain and Italy would go through to the semis and win on penalties. Then, I predicted that Spain would win overall with two or more goals.

It was quite a bold move to make such a specific prediction – there were so many different variables. In fact, the odds were 10,000–1 as they thought the chances of me getting it right were so slim. I placed a £1 accumulative bet with Paddy Power and then left my betting slip with ITV studios, in a secure locked box for two weeks, ahead of an appearance on *This Morning*.

As the tournament went on, one by one my predictions came true. Everything I'd seen in my mind became a reality. When the final came around Silva, Alba, Torres and Mata all scored for Spain, giving them a 4-0 win. I won £10,000!

I'd kept my prediction quiet. But when I went on the television show *This Morning* a couple of days after the final, they revealed what I'd put on the betting slip. It was a tense moment as Phillip Schofield opened the box to retrieve my betting slip. 'That's extraordinary,' said Phil as he read the results of my prediction. 'You can't fake something like that. It's incredible.'

Thank you for betting with **Paddy Power** BOOKMAKER

SELECTION: MEETING: TIME:

EURO 2012   (10,000/1)

1/4 FINAL WINNERS
PORTUGAL, GERMANY
SPAIN, ITALY (ON PENS)
SEMI FINAL WINNERS
SPAIN (ON PENS), ITALY
WINNER
     SPAIN (BY 2 OR MORE)

TOTAL STAKE   **PAYOUT**

£ 1 . 00 p   £   .   p

FULL INSTRUCTIONS ON THE REVERSE

DATE: 21/06/12 13:01:38
STAKE: £1.00

Visit PaddyPower.com

002 0854 02 52350003

Holly Willoughby was just as staggered. They just couldn't conceive how it was possible for me to be so accurate. It was another one of those moments where the gobsmacked looks on their faces made me beam with pride. The betting slip was later confirmed as genuine by Paddy Power.

When I collected my winnings, the bookies were just as shocked – they gave me that look I sometimes get from people where they eye me like I'm an alien from out of space or something. I knew exactly what I was going to do with the money, though; like my prediction there was no question about that. I gave the £10,000 to the Teenage Cancer Trust. I delivered the money myself to their hospital near Euston. It might sound like a huge sum of money, but really it's a tiny drop in the ocean for charities like those. But every donation counts and I was glad I was able to help. The charity works a lot more wonders than I do.

While I was at the hospital I had chance to hang out on some of the wards. One of the kids in there was really ill, but he had his own room, an Xbox and a big plasma TV, which the hospital had provided for him. He seemed as happy as Larry, even though he wasn't well at all. The extras that these charities provide really do make a huge difference. I know how important it is for kids to be cared for in hospital; they try to make the children's wards a home away from home rather than a scary, starched environment. They might not be at home, but the wards are painted in bright colours, there are sofas to hang out on, they have a playroom with Xboxes and DVD players. The children in the hospital might be incredibly ill, scared and homesick, but at least they have comforts to keep them distracted and entertained. You wouldn't believe the difference that makes.

I love doing those visits, but it can be a challenge for me, even though I probably understand as well as anyone what these kids are going through. I was in hospital for months at a time as a teenager and I know how scary it can be. But I don't always know what to do or say. When I visit, obviously I put on an apron and gloves so as not to pass on any germs. But then I'm thinking, *'Is it OK if they touch a card, when I ask them to choose one? Do I just get them to point?'* It's probably a silly thing to worry about, but because every child's case is different, I just never know.

Once I've worked out the best way to entertain them, the kids are a joy and it's brilliant to put smiles on their faces. I met the cutest little kid called Kieran recently. I was performing in the games room there and all the kids came in. This one kid sat there, with his drip, and he wore a bandanna as he'd lost his hair. He must have been about five years old and was pretty much ignoring me, playing FIFA on the Xbox. Then, all of a sudden, he paused the game and went, 'Who's the magician?'

I said, 'Me.'

'You don't look like a magician,' he pouted.

Halfway through the performance, he stopped me again and said, 'I like your adidas trainers. They're limited edition aren't they?' I was like, 'How on earth do you know about limited-edition adidas kicks? I only got them two days ago.' It was so random but I love things like that. All these kids might be desperately sick, but they're the sharpest, funniest little people you can meet.

It means the world to me that I can help them in different ways. Whether that's by raising money, raising the profile of the charities that do this brilliant work, or raising their spirits, I try to do everything I can.

It's all very well racing around in Ferraris in Singapore, but it's moments like this that put everything into perspective, and for once I'm the one who feels like I've been shown something genuinely magical. The spirit these kids have is beautiful. The human spirit is more powerful than anything I know.

CHAPTER 9

THE
MAGIC OF
TELEVISION

D espite all the whirlwind adventures Dan and I were having, the thing we wanted most just wasn't happening. Our own TV show. It was a weird scenario. It felt like we were rising to the top at 100mph, but the chance of making a proper TV series was travelling at 200mph – always out of our grasp. We couldn't get a show commissioned nor make enough money to fund our own show.

There were points between 2008 and 2010 when I was very, very down. I thought about all those years ago while I was recuperating in hospital, watching the film *Troy*. My moment of revelation. But sometimes, it felt like I'd never be able to impact the world through my magic the way I wanted to. And I couldn't see a way of getting any further.

I'd been on *Richard and Judy* and thought, '*This is it.*' I was presented an award by Will Smith, the biggest actor in the world, and thought, '*This is definitely it.*' Meeting Prince Charles, having the support of Coldplay, playing to 1.3 billion people at the EMAs, levitating Lindsay Lohan, appearing on Jonathan Ross... Every milestone I reached just didn't seem to take me any further than where I'd already been. I was on the cusp of achieving my ambitions, but I could never quite get past that tipping point. I was disillusioned. I was down. I was close to giving up. Close, but not quite.

The story of getting *Dynamo: Magician Impossible*, my first TV series, made is a long and convoluted one. But the way things finally worked out still mesmerises me.

Along the way I heard all sorts of things from the TV people. 'This kid's amazing, we're gonna make him a star!' 'Oh my God, how do you not have your own TV show already? Get this kid a series now.' Or, on a bad day, 'We really like you, Dynamo, but we just can't see how you're going to work.' I don't know what was worse: the flat refusals or the empty promises.

I'd read somewhere that Leonardo DiCaprio had over fifty auditions before he finally won a part in a major motion picture. I knew the Beatles' demo had initially been rejected by four different record labels. Will Smith had waited two years trying to hustle his way into a TV studio. Even my friend, Tinie Tempah, had been working for six years before he got a record deal.

But I was so disheartened.

Deciding to take fate into my hands, I decided to do everything possible to get my TV show – *The Art of Astonishment* as it was then called – made. I realised that a brand-new show reel could be the most important tool that I had. Because I'm a visual artist, and people want to see examples of my magic, I knew I had to make a show reel that would demonstrate exactly the type of TV programme that I wanted to make. If people didn't get my vision for my show, then I'd make it myself and prove my ideas were worthy of investment.

We compiled all the footage, everything we'd shot over the years – from the levitation I'd done in Singapore with Lindsay Lohan to my appearance on Jonathan Ross. It took Dan about four months to cut it, it was so painstaking. We treated it like we were making a TV show, even though it was only six minutes' long. But we'd seen other magicians' show reels and they weren't particularly inspiring. We wanted something that was engaging and well paced. So we spent a long time developing and creating what we thought would be the ultimate magician's show reel.

We took it to all the right places and showed it to all the right people, but no one was interested. Dan was good at keeping me positive, telling me that we had to keep going and we'd get there. And actually a lot of good things happened because of the show reel. I went to LA to hook up with Snoop Dogg to appear on his TV show, *Fatherhood*, which I filmed with his kids on Sunset Boulevard. I did Ashton Kutcher's *Aplusk* online show with Ashton and Kim Kardashian. I met with top Hollywood talent agents who were full of the whole 'We're gonna make you a star, kid' spiels. But ultimately, nothing came through. No one would give me a TV series.

I returned to London and went back to private gigs and hustling my way around nightclubs. I felt like I'd tried everything within my powers to succeed, but perhaps it was time to accept my lot in life.

Little did I know it then, but finally, things were about to change. A disastrous meeting, an auspicious dinner and a case of coincidence finally got us back on track.

One day, I was performing at a private party for a producer from Working Title Films who had worked on, among others, *Four Weddings and a Funeral*, *Fargo*, *Bridget Jones's Diary*, *Notting Hill* and so on. It was out in the countryside and you had extremely powerful media and political figures gathered, landing in helicopters and roaring up in the latest Ferraris and Porsches.

I did some magic for this guy called Nick and he was so into it. 'I need you to meet my wife', he said excitedly. Nick was married to a woman called Christa D'Souza, a journalist on *The Sunday Times*. 'She'll definitely want to interview you for the newspaper,' Nick said. So Dan and I, who were sharing a flat in north London at that time, invited them both round for dinner.

After the interview, I did some new magic that I was working on, and, once again, I blew them away, firstly by taking away Nick's strength, then by pushing Christa's phone into a bottle. Nick, who is the managing director of the theatre producer Cameron Mackintosh said, 'Look, Dynamo, what do you want to do? Where are you trying to take your magic?' I said, 'I want to make a TV show. It's called the *The Art of Astonishment* but we can't get funding. I want to integrate the magic I do with the story of my life so far and make a four- or six-part series. That's what I want to do.'

It turned out that Nick had a good contact at Universal Pictures. Before they left, we played them the show reel, which they loved, and Nick said he'd forward it to his contact. Pretty much straight away, Universal got in touch with us, offering us a distribution deal for a DVD. They said, 'We'd love to do something, but in order to do the DVD, you need to have a TV channel on board first.'

We were back to square one. It was really frustrating. We had a major DVD investor who was willing to put money in. We had all of the ideas and we had the knowledge of how to make a show that we thought could be a big hit. We had everything in place apart from a TV deal – that was the last piece of the puzzle. Dan went back to the same people we'd been talking to over the years – production companies, TV channels – pointing out that we had backing for the marketing and distribution of a DVD to accompany the series. There were no takers. We got the same old knock-backs with the same old excuses: 'We're just not sure it's a format that will work for us.'

♠

'OK, I have someone interested in potentially making a TV series with you guys. They don't have much budget, but maybe you can work something out'.

It was April 2010 and Dan had received a phone call from a contact connected with my Channel 4 show, *Dynamo's Estate of Mind*, back in 2006. It was a low-budget, one-off special that followed me around the country as I performed magic for everyone from Har-Mar Superstar to Coldplay. The meeting would be with a TV executive.

'What do you think, D? Is it worth it?' Dan asked. 'It turns out they have even less budget than the TV show we made four years ago.' He was concerned that this might be yet another waste of time, but I decided to try to stay optimistic. 'You know what? Let me just go and talk to them. I'll meet anybody, let me just see what they're saying.'

I had to go to a booking on the day of the meeting, so Dan went without me. The executive had a scruffy office in north London. The meeting started off badly, and went downhill from there.

'So, "Dynamo", right? I've never heard of him. Tell me what this guy's about,' said the exec, slouched in his chair, feet up on his desk. Given that I was fairly well known in TV circles, this came as a surprise to Dan, but he took it on the chin.

'I don't want to tell you too much about Dynamo, because I can't do proper justice to what he does,' he replied. 'I think it's better if you see what he's about.'

Dan set up the show reel on the guy's computer and it played through the big screen in his office. It opened with an incredible

I love social media.
I can stay in touch
with my followers
wherever I am

montage of Will Smith and Coldplay reacting to my magic, but when Dan looked over, the guy was twiddling with his BlackBerry. He wasn't even watching the screen. He looked up for a couple of seconds, looked back down, and kept on typing.

He ignored the show reel to the point that his screensaver kicked in. 'Mate, do you want to fix that?' asked Dan, as pictures of the TV executive's holiday whirred around the screen. 'Hmm, oh, yeah, yeah,' said the exec, absently touching the mouse. So far, he had paid about four seconds of attention to my show reel. He just sat there on his BlackBerry. At one point, he even left the room to talk to someone outside.

After six minutes of the guy barely tuning in the show reel ended. He turned to Dan. 'So, most people think magicians are assholes, what makes this guy so different?' The guy's rudeness and arrogance was actually almost comical. 'If you'd just looked at the show reel, then you might have some idea,' Dan retorted.

The exec got quite shirty about that; he really thought he was a big cheese. Taking a deep breath and masking his irritation, Dan explained to him that we wanted to make a show that comprised close-up magic with big stunts where we would have a big finish at the end of each one. What would make it different was that it would be a narrative-based show. It would be following me through my life and my attempts to share magic with the world. It would be about me as much as it would be about the magic. It was pretty much how *Dynamo: Magician Impossible* would turn out some two years later.

'Well, what kind of things does he do that would be interesting to film?' the exec yawned.

'Well, for instance, this week he'll be ringside at the David Haye fight,' Dan replied. Haye had just won the world title – he was a big deal and this was a huge sporting event.

'No, I don't think there's enough mileage in that,' the guy replied. 'I've got a better idea: we do a show where he does the tricks and then tells people how it's done. Like, he robs a jewellery store and then reveals how it's done. He...'

Dan couldn't bear to hear anymore. 'Look, let me just stop you there,' he interrupted. 'We're not interested in any of those ideas. We don't want to expose anything, that's not what we're about.'

At that point, the meeting pretty much ended. 'Well, I really hoped I'd see some cool stuff today but...' he shrugged. Dan just laughed. The person who had been the go-between and set up the meeting, was a little embarrassed at that point.

Dan stood up. 'I look after the greatest magician on the planet,' he said defiantly. 'I've got a six-figure deal with a major distributor on the table. Just because I've come to this meeting, don't be so naïve to think this is my only option.' And, with that, he walked out.

Truth be told, we didn't have anywhere else to go. But he wasn't about to let them know that.

♠

'How did it go?' I asked Dan when I saw him that evening, but he didn't need to answer. The look on his face said it all. It seemed like every door in the UK TV industry had been closed in our faces.

'Look, D, I've been thinking about this on the tube the whole way home,' he said. 'We're going to do this ourselves. We're going to raise the money ourselves – we're going to make the show ourselves. If we can only raise ten grand, we'll make a show for ten grand. If we can raise fifty grand, we'll make a show for fifty grand.'

I got really fired up. 'You know what, you're right. Let's go for it,' I smiled. 'We've got a bit of money in the bank; let's go hard on the private bookings, raise some more cash and hire our own crew. Forget everybody else. We know we've got a brilliant idea. Let's show people.'

We'd done Sports Relief a few months before, where I'd turned lottery tickets into cash for the charity for Davina McCall and Robbie Williams. The producer of Sports Relief was a man called Martin Dance who was a really nice guy, very supportive, and we had got on well. I always look out for people who I think are honest and straight talkers, people I think won't speak rubbish to me. I phoned him up. 'We want to make our own show and we want to make it independently. Will you come on board as a producer?'

It turned out that Martin was working at a TV production company called Phil McIntyre. What was interesting about that was that my first ever stage show, *An Audience with Dynamo*, had been promoted by Phil McIntyre. It was just a little show that I did in 2007 mostly for family, friends and my supporters.

Phil and Martin introduced us to a lady they were working with called Lucy Ansbro. It turned out that Lucy had worked in the same department at Universal that we were talking to about the DVD. It all seemed to be falling into place. We had a meeting with her, and got on really well.

'Can you help us pitch this programme?' we asked her. 'We've been shafted by a lot of production companies; we'd like to make this as a co-production with you and Phil. It's the only way we want to do it.' Fortunately, Lucy was fully up for it and she started to help us look for someone to make the series. She'd heard of at least one channel that might be interested.

Fashions in television come and go, and now channels had started looking for magic formats again. I was at the front of the queue.

This was around the same time that the BBC commissioned a series called *The Magicians*. I had been asked to do that, as well as two other similar formats that had been developed. But I always said that I only ever wanted to do my own programme. I didn't want to be a magician on a show in which I wasn't the main focus. Not because I'm arrogant or because I think I'm better than anyone else, but it was the vision I'd always had. And, I knew that doing those sorts of shows wouldn't further my magic. If you look at those series, it's hard to remember any of the magicians' names as individuals. No one knows who they are.

♠

Selling a magic show to a TV company is very difficult. It went a little bit like this:

'Hi, I'm Dynamo. I want to make this show where I'm going to walk on the River Thames. Then I'm going to fly from one building to another, walk through a window, and I'm going to predict the future, live, on Radio 1. Oh, I can't tell you how I'm going do it, but if you pay my company Inner Circle Films a certain amount of money, I'll make it happen!'

'So, what are we paying for, exactly?'

'Well... you're going to get all that. River Thames, teleportation, Radio 1...'

'Yes, but can you give us a breakdown of the money that you're expecting us to spend?'

'Well, due to the secretive nature of my magic I can't go into detail about what it's for. So, actually, no, I can't really tell you what I'm spending your money on, no...'

'Right. Er, right.'

The conversations always went that way, so it was a hard sell. Luckily, this was where my years of experience and hard work paid off. I don't think UKTV had ever seen a pitch like ours, because we had prepared for this for ten years. We were, if anything, over-prepared. By that point, because we were ready to do it ourselves, and were up for creating a pilot ourselves, we knew everything about the show. I knew what we wanted to do, down to the last detail. I was super-ambitious.

We also had an added incentive to dangle in front of them. 'By the way, Universal Pictures want to support the project.' So they're like, *'We've got this magician who's on the top of his game, he knows exactly what he wants to do, and he's already got Universal who want to put money into it, right from the off. This is a no-brainer.'*

They gave us the green light. Now we just had to actually make the show.

♠

Finally, after years and years, we had a deal. We were ready to sign on the dotted line. I was so excited, so happy, I couldn't believe it was happening.

We knew if the show didn't do well, we'd be screwed. If *The Art of Astonishment* was a flop, it would really impact on us all. Dan and I might never work again. Because of what we wanted to do – walking on the Thames, flying to LA etc., – we were spending so much money that no one else would ever be interested in us if the show wasn't a hit.

The original title, *The Art of Astonishment*, which was the title of a magic book by a magician called Paul Harris, also had to be

with hard work,
determination
and luck you can
defy the odds

One day this will all be mine!

Filming for BBC's *Inside the Human Body* on the Southbank.

Filming in Austria.

Smile for the camera!

Taking a magic power nap.

Finally finished filming!

Exploring the Chapéu Mangueira favela in Rio.

On the road again.

I want to share my

Me and Dan at Snowbombing.

Signing promo posters for *Dynamo: Magician Impossible*.

magic with the world

I seem to spend more time in the air than I do on the ground these days.

I wonder
if my life
has all
been an
illusion

changed. UKTV pointed out that the name was too long for the listings info that you get on your digital box as you're scrolling down to see what's on. They wanted something short and snappy, which we understood. Dan suggested *Magician Impossible*, a name that he'd mentioned to me a while ago. We thought it could work and the channel loved it.

We had a deal and we had a title, but that was just the start. Now we had to actually do what we said we would do. As always, we were making something out of nothing.

No pressure.

♠

We set up a small office space on Oxford Street and we squeezed everybody in there – director, producer, production crew, runners, the whole lot. After two weeks of preparation, we started shooting. We had a really good team, but no one had ever made a magic show like this, on this scale. There had never been one like it before in this country. All of us went in there pretty much unprepared, pretty much blind, but somehow sort of knowing what we wanted to do.

It was a gruelling seven months. The production period was crazy and the number of things that went wrong was just nuts. One of our crew members got mugged at gunpoint in Miami. My friend and driver from the show, Gilera, wrote off our car on our way to the Snowbombing festival in Mayrhofen, Austria. Then, the first time I tried to walk across the River Thames, disaster struck.

The heavens opened and there was torrential, end-of-the-world rain. I pretty much had my foot on the water, the covert cameras were set up to film, but it was raining so hard that no one was there to watch it. Without the reactions of passers-by, it wouldn't work. The magic would be lost.

The problem was, not only did we have to pay for an extra day's filming, but we only had one more day left in the schedule to film. The deadline for series completion was that weekend.

It was disaster after disaster.

But we all loved it – the team spirit kept us together. And thankfully the rain stopped, and the next day we got our shot.

When you make a TV series, there's pressure from the outset because there are so many external forces to take into account. You have to go out and film the same pieces of magic over and over because there are so many elements that need to go right simultaneously. You have to get a good reaction from the spectators, the camera guys need to capture the magic in the right way, the sound guy has to be happy and not have to stop everything because yet another low-flying plane overhead has disturbed the sound. There are so many different aspects that go into two minutes of screen time.

Even after we had finished most of the filming and knew we had some great stuff, the pressure didn't let up. When the TV ads came on to advertise episode one of *Dynamo: Magician Impossible*, we hadn't even finished making the show! We were literally filming and editing a week before the show went on air. But, somehow, we did it...

♠

At 9 p.m. on 11 July 2011, my first TV show *Dynamo: Magician Impossible* aired for the very first time. That evening I was doing a gig at the Savoy Hotel for an incredibly rich and powerful Russian heiress. I went off to the booking happily enough; I'd seen the show enough times in the edit suite and, because it was on the UKTV channel, Watch, rather than a terrestrial one, I wasn't expecting a huge number of viewers. I was just hoping we'd get some good feedback from anyone who had the chance to watch it.

As soon as I arrived at the Savoy, it quickly became apparent that the heiress's wealth and importance was vast. She and her family had flown in for the night from Russia, and their private jets were quite literally waiting on the runway to take them home after dinner. Every two minutes, yet another delivery would arrive; all of the major hotels and department stores were sending over extravagant gifts of flowers, champagne, jewellery and designer handbags. There were just sixteen people rattling around in this huge ballroom that was filling up with expensive luxury goods. They were all speaking Russian so I had no idea what they were saying, but their money talked loudly enough. This was wealth on a whole other level.

The gig was really fun; I went in, did my thing and the Russians loved it. I took one of the women's diamond rings. Before her eyes, I changed it into freezing cold ice and then melted it in front of them. They weren't sure whether to be angry or amazed because they didn't know if they were going to get it back or not.

I had been booked for two sets, and after the first, I went to a holding room where Dan was hanging out.

'D! Look at this,' Dan said excitedly, thrusting my phone under my nose. I was confused at first; he kept scrolling through the '@' messages in my Twitter timeline. 'But there's loads of them,' I said. He laughed. 'Hundreds!' Dan kept scrolling and refreshing and there was tweet after tweet after tweet. Not only were they coming at an alarming rate, but also literally each one read as if you had paid somebody to write the best possible thing that you could ever imagine. We watched as the number of followers started jumping up and then we turned to each other. 'I think we might have a hit,' grinned Dan.

Before I knew it, I had to go back and perform once more for the rich Russians, my mind buzzing with the implications of what Dan had shown me. Normally I'd get a handful of tweets a day; suddenly there was over a thousand. And from that moment, it was non-stop. My Facebook 'Likes' went from a few thousand to half a million. I went from approimately 70,000 followers on Twitter to 700,000.

The tweets were flying in from the likes of Tinie Tempah and Rio Ferdinand. Stephen Fry said the show was 'astonishing' and 'simply magnificent'. *Dynamo: Magician Impossible* quickly grew into somewhat of a phenomenon.

A week or so before the programme first aired, Dan and I had a meeting with the team at UKTV. 'So,' said Dan, 'what are your expectations for a show like this? What kind of viewing figures will you be hoping for?'

'What if we get a million?' I wondered aloud, cheekily.

The first-night viewing figures of *Dynamo: Magician Impossible* were 1.3 million. The highest Watch had had in their entire history was 738,000. We had smashed it. Not only did we exceed all expectations that day, but we bucked another trend. Normally a TV show has big first-night figures, which tend to drop off as the series continues. With *Dynamo: Magician Impossible*, the show built through social media and went viral – episode after episode attracted more and more viewers. Suddenly, we had this massive juggernaut. The first episode peaked at 1.5 million, with the numbers rising to 2 million people by the end of the series.

I can't describe how that feels. It was like the greatest bit of magic I'd ever performed. We'd made it happen. By ourselves. My family was so proud. After the first episode, Gramps cried tears of joy and my mum was so excited. She had a family fly all the way from Slovenia – the whole family – just so they could have their hair cut in her salon. She still gets random people who want to have Dynamo's mum cut their hair.

We couldn't really celebrate on that first night because we were stuck at the Savoy. But I always remember that as the moment where both Dan and I realised that everything was about to change.

♠

After the first episode aired, we were still filming the fourth episode as the schedule was running so late. I'm out on the street trying to record some stuff and around me everything is going nuts. Everything changed, literally, overnight. I couldn't film in the way that I used to, because people were just mobbing me. It was so bizarre, but completely brilliant.

When we were offered a second and third series, it felt like our hard work was finally paying off, although that brilliant offer brought a serious amount of extra hard work too. From July 2011 until Christmas Day 2011 I rarely took time off. I missed my family so much, after years of being so tight-knit it was hard. I missed Gramps especially. But we'd grab a phone call whenever we could and he loved hearing about my escapades. It was like he was living out some of his own dreams through me.

But we had to work hard if we were going to achieve the things we wanted. On the day before Christmas Eve, we flew out to Nigeria for a private show for a former Nigerian President. It was my first visit to Africa, and it was a real experience. We had no idea what to expect. When we landed, a man appeared after we had cleared customs and asked us for our passports. Reluctantly, we handed them over, not knowing if we'd ever see him or our passports again.

We were taken to a huge jeep with four armed security men; those guys rarely left our side while we were there, apart from when we went to sleep! We sped through the streets of Lagos, trying to take in the colours, smells and sights as we went. It looked like an amazing, energetic, crazy city, though we got to see hardly any of it. We were taken to a hotel, where we went straight to bed. I performed the next day and then we were put back in the jeep and taken to the airport. Thankfully, the man who had greeted us was there with our passports.

We hopped back on a plane, the streets of Lagos a blur, and arrived in London for Christmas lunch at Gordon Ramsay's house for his TV show. Boxing Day was the first day we had a chance to breathe and reflect. I drove up to Bradford to see my family and then on to Birmingham to spend time with my girlfriend before heading back to London in the early hours for a couple of hours' sleep. On 27 December, we were back to work.

There are many challenges when it comes to taking magic to television. There are only so many things you can levitate, for instance. You can levitate anything, but it's the ideas you run out of. You can levitate yourself, you can levitate a cup, you can levitate a chair, a person... What are you going to do next? How big is it going to get? Are you going to move the moon? How many things can you levitate? I'd rather look at doing something new than rehashing the same old stuff.

If you're a rapper or singer writing lyrics, to a certain extent you have an infinite toolbox. There are millions of different ways to rearrange words and there are different ways of delivering them – through various tones, levels, speeds, etc.

But with magic, you take one phone, you make it disappear. You take a cup, you make it disappear. If you do that back to back in a show, it's the same effect. It's no different in the spectator's eyes. Regardless of whether it's a phone or a cup, to the spectator it's essentially the same thing. The magician has made something vanish right in front of your eyes.

With series one of my TV show, *Dynamo: Magician Impossible*, there were around 100 effects – around twenty-five per episode. So 100 effects means 100 new pieces of magic that couldn't just be a repetition of the same one, but using a different object.

Twelve years of my ideas were thrown into series one, so the big challenge came with series two and three. I had a matter of months, not years, to create the magic for them. I've got to produce the same amount of material, with the same number of hours and airtime to fill, but with only six months of creativity feeding into it. Television eats material. When a stand-up comedian does an act for TV, he can't really use those same gags for his tour. Everyone's heard them already.

Obviously, there are certain things that I'll always do; they are associated with me and have become my speciality. A comedian has his own trademark delivery and in the same way, I'll have certain magic effects that are ascribed to me. The variations on the Polo mint appearance, levitating, walking through glass, moving tattoos and suntans about the body, and so on – they're all things that crop up regularly in my work.

Early on, one of my signature pieces of magic was pulling a Polo mint out of my neck. The first time I did it was on my second DVD, *Concrete Playground*, in 2006. I'd been doing two different things at that time and I joined them together. One of them was taking a necklace and sawing into my neck, and the other one was taking somebody's ring, or a Polo, swallowing it, and making it disappear and then reappear on the same chain.

I decided to combine the two ideas, because I always thought that sawing my neck captured people's attention, but it didn't really have any purpose. So I thought if I swallow the Polo, saw the necklace into my neck, and then cause it to appear back on the necklace, then the illusion goes full circle.

I always try to tell a story with my magic; there has to be a journey and there has to be a purpose.

I have a few other specialties, of course, but I like to constantly mix things up. For example, in the first series of *Dynamo: Magician Impossible*, one of the things people talked about were the different levitations, using both myself and inanimate objects. In the second series, I did something called a suspension in Rio; I balanced on a bench just using my hand. Suspension is different to levitation; it's about balance rather than floating. There was the magic that I did with The Stone Roses frontman Ian Brown's guitars, where I suspended a guitar on a chair. In the second series I did it with mobile phones. I've tried to touch on certain things but do them differently each time. So there are similarities, there's continuation, but there's also progression.

In the second series, I taught people, so to speak, how to put the phone inside the bottle. Everyone always asks me about the phone in the bottle, so I explain how to do it: I borrow someone's phone, wave it and it shrinks to a miniature version of the phone, and then I can drop it into the bottle. When it's in the bottle, I shake it, and it grows back to its normal size again inside the bottle, and I pass it back to them. That's my 'explanation'.

After series one aired, I really listened to what people were saying – what they liked, what they didn't, the magic that really enthralled them and the magic that they weren't so taken by. I've tried to play on the talking points and pick the types of magic that everyone really loves.

I get ideas for new magic everywhere. It used to be that I would be inspired on the bus or tube, though I can't get them so much these days. Nowadays it's riding around in my car, other times when I'm at the office. I won't lie; the toilet is often a good place of inspiration for me too. The best way, though, is usually through chatting to random strangers. For some reason, people talk to me and finding out what people like gives me inspiration. I used to put coins into bottles, and then one night, some guy goes, 'Do that with my phone.' I was like, 'OK,' and I put his phone in a bottle. It's been one of the most talked-about things I've ever done. A fan gave me a fantastic idea recently. He told me the best thing I've heard in a long time and it's something that I'm working on as I write.

One thing that I try to do to stand out and progress is to embrace popular culture and modern technology. I took my magic to the DVD format, then to MySpace and from there to YouTube and Twitter. I was the first person to perform magic over Twitter, which I got Snoop Dogg involved in. I guessed which card he was thinking of. I guessed the three of diamonds correctly, otherwise that would have been embarrassing, with our combined ten million followers. Similarly, it was important for me to have an app for *Dynamo: Magician Impossible* while the show was on air. It's about embracing the ever-changing world that we live in.

For me, it's essential for both forming ideas and keeping my content fresh. If you don't keep up, you get left behind.

♠

Since I was a teenager, I've studied the art of magic. The thoughts and theories have changed a lot over the last few years. Some people don't believe that magic can be simplified. They think it's much more of a fluid thing. There are many different types of magic.

You've got 'appearance', which is making things appear. One of my favourite moments from the second series was the scene in episode one with my nan. I did her crossword for her in about two seconds – I made the words appear in a flash. As usual she wasn't impressed. 'Oh yeah, I see,' she nodded nonchalantly. One of these days I'll do something that will really impress her!

'Disappearance' is obviously the opposite. You've seen me make coins disappear and reappear all over the place. In the second series, I even made myself disappear after a crowded event at an HMV store, leaving just a pile of clothes behind.

'Penetration' is passing one object through another. For example, when I push someone's phone into a beer bottle. Another example is when I walked through glass in front of Rio Ferdinand. I penetrated through the glass and appeared on the other side of the window.

'Transposition' occurs when two things change places. This might happen when I, for example, take Coca-Cola and swap it with Sprite. This goes right back to the first magic trick Gramps showed me where you make red and green matches switch boxes.

The magic that has made a lot of headlines are my predictions. There was the thing I did with the Euro 2012 bet, but I've also used this when predicting the news on Scott Mills's Radio 1 show.

I went to the Radio 1 studios a few days before with a locked and sealed safety-deposit box. I gave it to Scott and told him not to open it or try to tamper with it in any way. Two days later, I returned to the studios and live on Scott's show I asked him to go through the pile of newspapers that were in the studio. I asked him to pick one and choose a positive, uplifting story that he felt compelled to read on air. He chose the *Metro* from that day (20 July 2011) and, after rifling through the paper, he finally picked out a story about a record-breaking mountaineer who had scaled Everest three times. 'We've a lot to be proud of,' read the headline.

At that moment, I announced that I had somewhere to go and I took off, leaving him with the key to the box. After I left, Scott opened the safe and inside was a sketch, drawn by me all those days before. It was of the very same story he had chosen and I'd drawn it as it was laid out on the newspaper page. I'd written the headline 'A lot to be proud of' and sketched the mountaineer in his red jacket with his ski goggles on his head and so on. Scott and his team were dumbfounded.

I've always done predictions with my friends just for fun. We'd make a little wager on things and over the years I got quite good at it. I have quite a sharp memory, so I use memory and mathematics to think, '*OK, this is going to be the outcome of this event.*'

It is risky doing predictions because once you commit to it, you can't change your mind. Lots of times, my magic doesn't always work out how I had envisaged it in my head, but I can easily freestyle my way out of it. I have so many ideas to hand; I rarely know what I'm going to do at a gig anyway. Lots of times I use props on the spot or even create new magic as I go along.

With predictions, however, there's no freestyling your way out of trouble. I don't really like creating too much hype either. I prefer

London 2012 Torch Relay

We've a lot to be pro...

P

to let the magic be strong enough on its own, and then the hype comes anyway. But with predictions, the minute you leave an envelope with someone and say, 'All right, that's the prediction in there, open it in a week,' then you have expectation building for a whole week. If they open the envelope and the prediction is wrong then you're left standing there looking ridiculous.

I've only really done two major predictions in my life: the newspaper article sketch on Scott Mills's radio show and the Euro 2012 accumulator bet.

For me, predictions are more nerve-racking than walking on water, but the predictions I've done have gone amazingly well. I think they add to the legacy I'm trying to create and they fit in with my style. I would never do something that's not me just because it's an impressive piece of magic. I'm very careful that I am consistent in who I am and what I do.

♠

People often ask me why I think the first series of *Dynamo: Magician Impossible* was such a success. I've thought about it quite a lot.

One difference with the show, and this is a really important thing, was that we didn't want to pre-promote what I was going to do. Every other magic show announces its intentions: 'I'm going to do this; you're going to be amazed.' And when you do that, you build expectations.

With the River Thames, we didn't tell anybody what was happening. I went down to the river at 9.30 p.m. and just started walking. The bystanders who were there were people who just happened to be walking past. We didn't advertise or promote it; we just did it.

A few days later, pictures of me standing in the middle of the river in my bright red jacket started to emerge online. Within an hour, it had gone global, with the story cropping up in Australia, India, Germany and South Africa. I watched it spread around the world overnight. People could feel the authenticity, so we got people's interests piqued straight away. It was mad seeing news articles come up online in languages from countries I'd never even been to.

Television has lost a key demographic; generally speaking, it has lost its young audience. Because the whole industry is fragmented, there are far fewer people watching each television channel, there is far more competition, advertising space is worth less, and I think because of that, the quality has been pushed down. The cost of making television programmes is high, so they're obviously very careful about what decisions they make, but some are not in tune with current trends. No one wants to take a risk on the unknown and unproven.

So I think that the other, really pertinent reason for the success of *Dynamo: Magician Impossible* was that we were making a show that was relevant. Yes, it's a magic show, but the music we were choosing, the people who were in it, the places we were going to and my own story was relevant to people in my age group. I was talking to my peers in a way that they could understand and relate to, and in a way that no other show was really doing.

Not only that, we weren't producing it on the cheap. It wasn't like, 'Oh, here's a little niche thing for you guys.' This was a proper, big-budget TV series that felt like a movie. I said from the outset that I wanted to give people something of real value; that for me is always the starting point. The amazing thing is, as I think *Dynamo: Magician Impossible* has shown, once you create a show that has that quality and that detail, then you stand a good chance. We really put ourselves on the line, because we could have lost a fortune by approaching it that way.

There was nothing else like *Dynamo: Magician Impossible* on television. Because of the way programmes are commissioned, we were lucky we got through the door – there are many brilliant people out there who could be doing similar things, but they aren't able to get their first break.

As soon as people saw that *Dynamo: Magician Impossible* was a hit, every channel that had turned us down in the past started to come back. But I didn't want to seem like I was just jumping ship. 'Thanks for the money, thanks for believing in me, thanks for everything, but I'm off to a terrestrial channel.'

I didn't want to give the impression I was selling out. I had formed a good relationship with UKTV, and I had also been granted a certain amount of creative freedom. We also realised that we were by far the biggest thing on that channel. We were *The X Factor* or *Big Brother* of UKTV. And that's a very rare position to find yourself in. If I had gone to a bigger channel, I'd be right down the pecking order. I would rather be at the top of that chain than further down it.

The second series of *Dynamo: Magician Impossible* was an even greater success; our viewing figures hit the 2.1 million mark, becoming Watch's biggest-ever television show and the third most-watched show in its time slot – including the terrestrial channels.

Now, of course, when you get a big hit like ours then suddenly you find that everyone else starts trying to replicate its success by commissioning magic shows. But what they don't realise is that it's not a gimmick. It's not just about having somebody who's kind of cool doing magic. It's about the ten, fifteen years of work that I put in to really understand my craft. It's about the thought behind it; it's the story behind it. You can't just fake it.

I hope now that TV production companies might change their approach to making programmes a little bit. It might actually open the door to other new talent, because it's a shame that television can be so conservative.

I have learnt a valuable lesson on this journey. Having a successful show with huge viewing figures is one thing. But knowing that what you do brings joy to people is a completely different matter. Now I've achieved, finally, what I set out to achieve, it's about what I can do for other people. I'm in a position now where I can make a difference.

I can't describe how it feels. We made it happen

CHAPTER 10

SOUNDTRACK OF MY LIFE

've walked on water, thrown myself down an eighty-foot building, I've walked through walls, disappeared into thin air and turned snow into diamonds. Snoop freestyling about me was the coolest moment, while walking across the Thames was a pivotal event and walking down the *Los Angeles Times* building was the scariest. But one of the highlights of my career is the time I used my magic on Tinie Tempah.

It was November 2010 and Tinie was playing in Manchester. Before he did his show, I headed backstage to give him one of my own.

'Yo! Mr D, what's going on? You made it down, come in, come in,' said Tinie, ever the gracious host, welcoming me into his dressing room. 'This is the best magician in the world,' Tinie told his boys. He yelled at all his mates to come into the dressing room.

Once they'd all piled in, I made Tinie pull a chain through my neck. 'Oh my God,' he laughed, looking a bit disturbed at having to then touch the same chain. Next, I told him I wanted to do something else.

'I know it sounds silly, but every time I see you, I never get you to sign anything,' I said. 'I know you've signed thousands of CDs, but I'd like to get mine signed.'

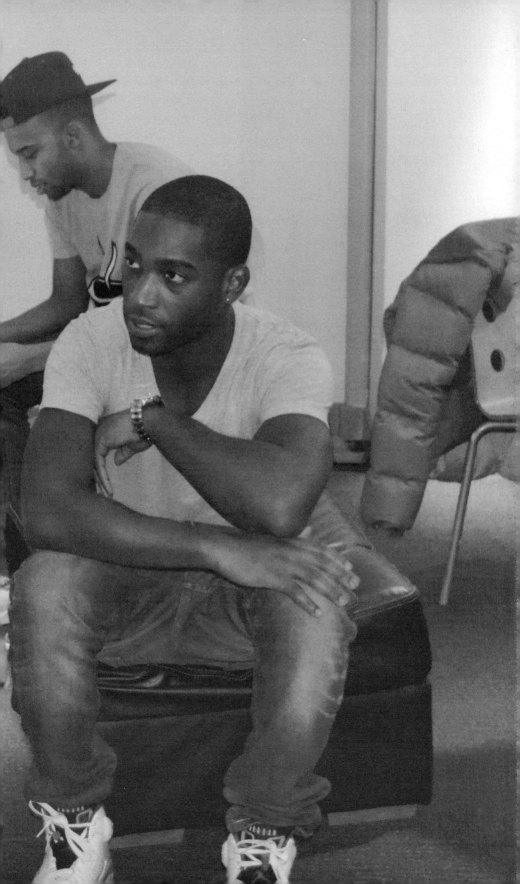

'Cool,' he replied. 'Let's do it.' I produced the CD and showed it to him.

'You've signed loads of them so I want mine to be a bit special. I want to see your eyes,' I said.

On the cover of his album *Disc-Overy*, Tinie is staring into the camera, but his eyes are covered by a pair of dark shades. I held the CD, rubbed the case and took Tinie's sunglasses clean off.

He actually dived into the wardrobe. 'That picture doesn't even exist, Bruv! He took the glasses off of my eyes and moved them onto my forehead!' he shouted, jumping around in astonishment. I had taken the album cover, and, in front of his face, removed his sunglasses to reveal his eyes and created a one-of-a-kind Tinie Tempah album.

It's the one moment in my magic career that still stands out as the most memorable. There are a lot of reasons why. His reaction was incredible; it got amazing feedback from viewers and for me it felt like Tinie and I were two people on the top of their game doing something great. I finally had my own TV show; he'd been to number one with 'Pass Out' and had won BRIT Awards. He was a huge star.

I had the idea to do the album illusion on the very same day. On the drive up to Manchester, I pulled out his CD, and I was like, *'Let me see. Could I do something with his lyrics? Could I do something with his songs?'*

I looked at the album cover and I was like, *'He's always wearing glasses, maybe I should do something with them... Yeah, that could be cool.'*

So I called Dan, and said 'What do you reckon about this?' and he replied, 'I'd have to see it, but it sounds all right.' Three hours later, we were in Manchester doing it.

I love Manchester – it's such a vibrant city, and I love the northern humour, I guess because I'm a northerner myself. There's no messing about with Mancunians – they say what they think. It might rain all the time but the streets are always full of life and energy. The centre was heavily regenerated after the 1996 IRA bomb, so the city feels very modern and buzzing, and it's full of brilliant little bars and clubs around the old canals.

It's also one of those places that have a huge musical heritage. There are so many cool groups that come from there – Oasis, Happy Mondays, The Stone Roses, The Buzzcocks, The Smiths, Joy Division, New Order... even The Bee Gees and Take That! You have to respect a city that can produce that number of groundbreaking bands. I have a very eclectic taste in music: everything from rap and R&B to indie and pop. In fact, music has landed me in the most random of situations at times.

♠

In 2006, I was honoured when Damon Albarn, who had seen me do my magic backstage at a Blur show, asked if I would open for his new band, The Gorillaz, at New York's Harlem Apollo Theatre.

The band was doing five nights at the Apollo for the *Demon Days* album. They invited all the artists who were on the album to perform, so you had everyone from Shaun Ryder (Happy Monday's lead singer) and Ike Turner, to Dustin Hoffman doing the intro, to my mates De La Soul on the song, 'Feel Good Inc.'. Every single collaborator from the album turned up. It was epic.

After one of the performances, I sat outside the back of the
Apollo with Shaun and Damon, just chatting about the show,
New York, life in general. They were smoking and we were
hanging out. It was mad – we had a normal conversation, which
you wouldn't expect to have with those kinds of guys. They're
rock-and-roll stars. At one point, though, things weren't so
normal – Damon pulled a stone from his pocket, drew a circle on
my head and kissed me on the head. It was a bit odd, but it's
Damon Albarn, what are you going to do?

I got a totally different view of New York on that trip. As well as
doing all the sightseeing that I hadn't had a chance to do on my
previous visit, I also spent time in the historic area of uptown
Manhattan. Harlem has produced music greats from Billie
Holiday to P. Diddy. Historically, it might have been a violent
place, but it is rich in music, dance, art, literature and theatre.
Nowadays, it's quite upmarket; there are organic shops and
macrobiotic cafes, and it's been heavily regenerated. Back when
I visited, though, it was still a little bit lively.

Through De La Soul, I had hooked up my friend, Luti, to film a
video for De La's Maseo, who had signed a new artist to his label.
We were waiting for him to arrive and we ended up at Rucker
Park, which is a famous court where the street basketballers go.
It's the best b-ball you'll ever see. I think these guys are better
than the highly-paid professionals.

When they first saw the cameras they were like, 'What's going on
here?' because we had a big crowd and it looked a bit dodgy. But
once they saw what we were doing, and that we weren't filming
anything that was going to make them look bad, they loved it. I
did a bit of magic for them and they were buzzing.

I remember one of these guys gave me a one-dollar bill and I
changed it into a twenty. As soon as I did, he ran straight into a

nearby shop. 'I spent it before you changed it back,' he laughed on his return.

About forty minutes later, we were in a completely different part of Harlem. Some random guy comes up to me and he goes, 'Hey, are you the magic guy?' I'm like, 'Yeah...' So he goes, 'Change my dollar into a twenty, change it into a twenty!' The news had spread throughout Harlem. I just laughed, because you could tell he was serious, but it was funny as well. It was just weird to see how fast news had travelled through Harlem like that. I was reminded once more that magic is a powerful thing.

I wasn't scared to be in Harlem. If I'd been nervous on my first trip to New York, I wasn't on this occasion. I do find that, for some reason, I'm fine around people who others generally feel uncomfortable with. Maybe because I'm a bit different myself. I can relate to those people. I can appreciate growing up in that situation and not having any opportunities, so I can see why people might go the way that they do.

Obviously, now I have a luxurious lifestyle, but growing up things were very different. I can't imagine what it would have been like to have had everything given to me on a plate.

I went to New York to hang out with Damon Albarn, but I actually had the best time on the streets of Harlem.

♠

I'm lucky to have made friends with some of music's greats. From Ian Brown from The Stone Roses and De La Soul, to Tinie Tempah and Snoop, I've found myself hanging out with some super-cool guys in the most random of scenarios. Not only that, but I've been involved in music quite a bit, albeit in a roundabout way. Sway rapped about me in his song 'Still Speedin'', and I've appeared in music videos for Dizzee Rascal,

Example, SAS (which also featured a then-unknown Kanye West) and The Raconteurs.

The Raconteurs' video for 'Hands' was just random. Jack White's people called me up and said, 'We want you to do this.' I was like, 'OK, cool.' I nearly missed the opportunity to do that video, though. It was being shot in Oslo, so I headed to the airport the morning before, nice and early. It was only at check-in that I realised my passport was out of date. I had to cancel that flight, jump in the car with Dan and peg it down to Peterborough to get an emergency passport. We got there, waited in the massive long queue, and as we went to leave, the car decided to break down.

The video was being shot early the next morning, so I had to get a flight that night. We left the car, jumped on a coach, a train and in a taxi, and finally got back to Heathrow with about ten minutes to spare. It was so close, we almost didn't make it!

I eventually got to Oslo and I realised that I was the main feature in the video. I was like, 'Whoa!' The next thing you know, it's all over the internet and on the TV. It was such a different crowd for me and it gave me a new market. I remember Zane Lowe came up to me at a festival not long after the video dropped. I'd never met him before, and he was like, 'Yo, Dynamo, I've got to get you on *Gonzo*. I loved you in The Raconteurs' video.' Of all the things he could have seen me in, that's where he spotted me.

I think the indie kids like me. Since that video I've done magic at the *NME* Awards and performed for the Arctic Monkeys. Another time I was kidnapped by the Kings of Leon. It was after we'd been on Jonathan Ross together; when the Kings come calling, you can't say no.

I'd been trying to get onto Jonathan Ross for a while. In the end, Dan and me sent a showreel to Jonathan Ross's company, Hot Sauce, and they came back and booked me. It was quite a surprise. I got an opportunity to go on the show, very out of the blue, even though I didn't really have anything to promote at that point.

I'd been in hospital the day before with my Crohn's, so it was touch and go whether or not I could do it. But I pulled it together, and despite feeling pretty rough doing filming, I went and did what I had to do.

Kings of Leon and the Bond girl Ursula Andress were my fellow guests. After I'd done my thing, the Kings invited me to a party that night. So I went. I had lots of fun showing them and their mates some magic and hanging out. As we left, Jared pulled me aside and said, 'We're off on tour tomorrow, do you want to come with us?' I asked Dan if I was free to go, he said yes, and I was away for two weeks.

It was wicked fun; I loved hanging out with them as a band. We went all over the UK. They'd do their music and I'd do my magic for them and the fans. It was pretty rock and roll – but one lesson I've learnt along the way is this: what happens on tour, stays on tour!

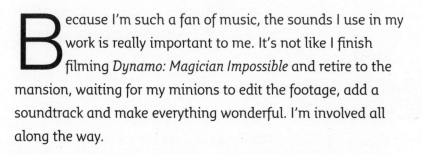

Because I'm such a fan of music, the sounds I use in my work is really important to me. It's not like I finish filming *Dynamo: Magician Impossible* and retire to the mansion, waiting for my minions to edit the footage, add a soundtrack and make everything wonderful. I'm involved all along the way.

Me, Dan, everyone in the team – we all throw a few ideas in. It's a combination of what we're listening to at the moment, or songs we know of that make us think. It has to be something that suits the magic, but doesn't distract from it either. We picked a Dead Weather tune called *I Can't Hear You* recently for a piece of magic in Las Vegas, where I make a car vanish whilst I'm doing doughnuts in it. It was in the middle of the desert, on this random dirt track where all the drifters go. The Dead Weather tune fit so perfectly because the music's so hard. Some sequences work best when you have an electronic sound; some of them need to have that raw, real feel using guitars, like the noise of an engine revving. It really adds to the moment.

The music we feature is not always stuff that I like necessarily. Some of it is, but a lot of the times we choose it because it's authentic to the place where the magic is situated. Obviously, in Brazil we really researched a lot of the local music. In the end, we actually found a South American drummer who provided the best soundtrack for us. It's partly about authenticity; and partly about pacing, or it can be something that helps to tell the story. For me one of the things that worked really well in series one was Massive Attack's 'Teardrops', which we used for an impossible body suspension.

For the River Thames, we used Linkin Park's 'Crawling'. It isn't the same without that song.

We always do a test-run, and if the music stands out, it's a bad thing. Because you actually want to almost forget the music is there, so that it gels perfectly with the scene. Often we'll try loads of things, and sometimes one song just fits. We definitely spend a lot of time making sure that it's right.

We also try to include different music and genres. For me, the soundtrack was always about having something that felt timeless. So we'll have a mix of modern music that I'm into – like the instrumental of Kano's 'Spaceship' – but then we'll also go back to a lot of classics. In series two, episode one, of *Dynamo: Magician Impossible*, we used the O'Jays and at the start of the series we used Dinah Washington's 'What a Difference a Day Makes'. For me, everything has a history to it, and there's no future without the past. Even though my demographic is a relatively young one, all of that modern music has come from somewhere. It's nice to give the series that classic feel.

As a film fanatic, I'm aware that directors like Martin Scorsese and Quentin Tarantino have amazing music scores because they are music addicts. I've read all the interviews with Tarantino about the record choices that he put in his films. Tarantino has the most incredible rare record collection, all organised into genres and sub-genres; it's an astonishing library of music. I remember Scorsese talking about *Goodfellas*, too. There's a shoot-out scene that is underscored with Eric Clapton's 'Layla'.

He said that the reason he used such a poppy tune is because when he grew up, that's what would have been playing then in his locality, even though it wasn't particularly dramatic. Watching this scene taught me that sometimes things look more exciting if you have a contrasting or understated soundtrack. So we play around with the music in *Dynamo: Magician Impossible* constantly to keep it feeling really natural.

There's another technique we use – there's actually a name for it – 'diegetic sound'. It's when the only sounds you hear on screen are natural ones coming from the action itself, in other words there are no sound effects or music added later. For example, you might have music that's coming out of a car radio or a shop in the background rather than being played as a soundtrack over the top of the scene. If you've seen *The Wire*, pretty much all the music in that show comes from organic sources, like people on the street. There's no score, apart from the theme tune. When we first came up with the idea for *The Art of Astonishment*, as *Dynamo: Magician Impossible* was then known, we talked about having the music coming from buskers and other organic sources. The idea was to make the magic feel as real as possible. However, for various reasons, including technical ones, we decided in the end to go with a soundtrack.

I think there are a lot of people out there making TV who perhaps don't have the same attention to detail when choosing music. They'll use the same songs that everyone else goes for. People have been so complimentary about our choice of music. 'It's amazing that you're not using Katy Perry,' someone said to me once. We did actually use Katy Perry, to be fair, but only in the right place...!

Our challenge with *Dynamo: Magician Impossible* was to make something really special, both visually and aurally arresting, like a movie but on a TV budget. I like to think the viewing figures proved we succeeded.

CHAPTER 11

THE LOOK ON PEOPLE'S FACES

'What? What? How did you do that? Oh my GOD, tell me, how did you do that?!'

As David Blaine proved early on with his television series, *Street Magic*, the most important part of any magic show is the spectator. With television, everyone expects camera trickery, CGI, Photoshop and special effects. So the thing that sells the magic itself, that really proves to people that what they saw was real and not camera trickery, is the reaction of the spectator. If you don't believe the reactions of the people you are watching, then the whole thing is a mockery and the show would lose credibility.

With YouTube, Instagram, Photoshop, the internet and so on, people are a lot savvier. When I was a kid I didn't question the fact that Superman could fly around the world so fast that it could make the world spin the other way, despite the clunky special effects. It didn't occur to me that it wasn't real. Nowadays, though, kids want everything CGI-laden and in 3D. They know, from a much younger age, that what they're watching is a film. Sure, they don't care – it's film, a fantasy – but they're too technologically clued up to believe in it. So it's my job to bring back that childish innocence and wide-eyed wonder, and show that magic is real and not about CGI and camera tricks.

Over the years, the biggest change in magic has been the fact
that it has moved from the stage and theatre where people
always used to see it, with elaborate props and huge sets,
and it is now being brought directly to the people on the street.
Nowadays, we have everything available to us at the click of a
button; we watch films and live-stream concerts on our phones;
we certainly don't need to go to a theatre to see a live
performance. As a result, it's much harder for magic shows to
put bums on seats like they used to. Even when you do, you're
not hitting the size of audience in a theatre in the way that you
can online. I can post a video of me doing magic on the street, in
a club – anywhere – and with a matter of days, or even less, over
a million people will have watched it. No need to book an
expensive theatre and waste energy trying to sell tickets.

I've had to be inventive when it comes to getting and keeping
people's attention. When I am creating my show, I need to prove
that I'm not using camera effects or Photoshop or CGI in my work.

What you see on your television set is what you'd see if you were with me on the street. I have to rely wholly on the spectator to help me convince the viewer that what they're watching hasn't been tampered with. It's just me, the spectator and the magic.

With *Dynamo: Magician Impossible*, I can spend eight hours of the day trying to film one piece of magic, which equates to only three minutes of airtime. The reason it takes so long is because I don't want to have that 'set-up' feel. You have to be very, very patient to make a show like mine.

Over the years, I've witnessed some of the best reactions at festivals. People are basically on holiday – they're relaxed, their defences are down and they are actively looking to be entertained. You're almost guaranteed a good response. Because the festival audience has been a part of my career since day dot, I wanted to incorporate that into my first series of *Dynamo: Magician Impossible*. But, rather than go to your typical festival though, I fancied doing one with a difference. Snowbombing in Mayrhofen, Austria, is renowned for being the biggest, craziest festival in the snow. There's live music, snowboarding, DJs, drinking and, in 2011, everyone from Mark Ronson to Fatboy Slim, The Prodigy and Professor Green were playing there. It's one big rave up a mountain.

As they sponsor the festival, Volvo lay on cars for artists, guests and journalists to travel there in a kind of Gumball Rally. My film crew, my boys and I all set off together. The first day we drove from Maidstone to Frankfurt and then the next day we headed for Mayrhofen, which was a good five-hour drive. Along the way we managed to have ourselves a little crash. I was actually asleep at the time. In fact, I didn't wake up until the police arrived to make sure we were OK. I find it hard to get to sleep, but when I eventually nod off there's no waking me! I slept through the entire thing. Gilera had managed to write off the poor Volvo but, thankfully, no one was hurt and we managed to hitch a ride to the resort.

It was my first time in a ski village, but as I was filming I wasn't allowed to ski. Not because we didn't have time, but due to our insurance policy. I couldn't afford to break a leg or do anything that would jeopardise the show. It was so annoying. I'd go up to the top of this mountain, every day, to film magic and I wouldn't be able to ski. I'd have to get the lift back down again. Next time I get chance, I want to go back and try snowboarding.

Other than the fact there would be no extreme sports for me, the experience was amazing. I felt like I was doing magic on top of the world. I've never seen views like it in my life – the brilliant blue skies and dramatic snow-capped peaks were like something from a postcard. The air up there is so fresh too; I felt invigorated and full of energy.

I hadn't planned what I would do at Snowbombing. Obviously, I expected there to be lots of snow, so I had some vague ideas, but I prefer to go to a place, have a look around, see what's there, and find some inspiration. Sometimes I pre-plan, but not everything looks as good as you think it will in real life. I probably went to Austria with ten or so specific ideas and ended up thinking of over five more while I was there.

It's like a musician who goes into a studio and probably makes fifty songs for an album but only picks the best eleven. Similarly, I might not get the reactions I need from the magic that I do, so we have to filter the resulting footage and decide what will, and won't, make the final cut.

Now, the thing with Snowbombing is that people's reactions were never too quiet or shy – quite the opposite. Most of the time they were a bit too, er, enthusiastic, so we ended up not being able to use that footage. People really do go crazy up on that mountain – I swear some people partied straight through for the whole five days! There was a guy up there who walked around constantly wearing a horse's head. He couldn't give much of a physical reaction, but it made a great piece of television regardless.

We eventually managed to find two girls who were not only enthusiastic, but who also responded perfectly to the magic I had planned. I had noticed them up on the top of the mountain and I decided there and then to use what was around me to make something magical happen.

I asked them to touch the snow and they concurred that it was very cold and that it was actual snow. I then turned on my magic breath, breathed on the snow and handed the 'snow' back to them. It had turned into diamonds. 'What? What? How did you do that?' they laughed.

Seeing as diamonds are a girl's best friend, my magic of choice seemed like a nice way to break the ice (no pun intended).

Sometimes a piece of magic might not turn out how I envisioned, or we might not capture it in the best way on camera. More importantly, though, you can't guarantee someone will react in the way you want, just because it makes good television. Sometimes, people will give the impression they're not bothered by what they've seen, but it's just because they're gobsmacked and their brains are still trying to process it. Some people will literally have their jaws open, staring wildly in disbelief, but that doesn't work as well for television. Sometimes us Brits can be a bit reserved and that doesn't help us convey what has happened either. That's partly why we have travelled the world with the series, to show the wide-ranging reactions that magic can provoke, depending on where you go.

Nothing beats the feeling of seeing someone's eyes widening, their mouth opening and the look of amazement on their face. When we filmed *Dynamo: Magician Impossible*, we just embraced all of the weird situations that life threw up – a car crash, a horse's head and drunken snowboarders – because no matter how much you plan things, life always takes its own path.

♠

I think one of the best – or at least most memorable – reactions I've had happened years and years ago. I did an event at a club called Pennington's in Bradford, which doesn't actually exist anymore. It was a friend of a friend's birthday and my mate Marcus asked me if I fancied going along to do some magic. We rocked up, hung out, and as it got busier, I started to do my thing. The crowd got bigger and bigger, with everyone trying to get a good view. I decided to chill out for a bit, but then this guy goes, 'Please show my girlfriend something, she couldn't see what you were doing before.' The thing was, what I did wasn't even anything big. I just bent my finger in half, and the girl fainted. I mean, totally out for the count. She hit the deck and stayed there. I didn't know what to do, I was so shocked myself. In the end, we poured water on her face to wake her up. She was a bit freaked out, so I offered to do some card magic on her. 'No, no, no thank you, I'm fine,' she mumbled and her boyfriend took her off, mouthing a 'sorry' as he went.

It's funny how magic can affect people in radically different ways outside of the traditional reaction. Of course, I love it when people are like, 'Wow, great,' but then you'll get someone like Snoop Dogg who just randomly did a rap about me. And then there was the Will Smith moment where he changed his speech at The Prince's Trust event; I find it amazing the way my magic can provoke a reaction in someone and cause them to do something neither of us expected. It's crazy.

Of course, not everyone likes magic and sometimes you have to deal with negative reactions. If people are drunk they can get a bit gobby and that's never cool. Everyone's got an opinion when they've had a few, although I think I've got better at spotting those people and making sure I avoid them these days. I've been doing magic in nightclubs for years now, so I can usually tell if someone's going to give me grief.

Depending where you are in the world, magic is viewed very differently. In Haiti, magic is seen as a powerful and real force. People there practise voodoo and, if used to ill effect, it's believed to bring great harm and even death to people. Whenever I've done magic on Haitian people, they get very, very freaked out. There was a time in Miami where I pulled a can of Coke out of my shoes. The guy I did it on, a coconut seller, literally grabbed his trolley and ran off down the street. I mean, sprinted. Similarly, Wyclef Jean from the Fugees, who is also Haitian, did the same thing – his eyes widened in shock and off he ran!

I love that no matter who it is I'm performing for, I can provoke a totally natural, often uncontrolled, reaction. And every response is different. One time when I pulled a Polo out of my neck, Pharrell Williams, basically the coolest guy on the planet, ran off screaming. Then I stole his bank details and he literally went pale. I really think he thought I was going to take his money!

I've found that in London you always get the best reactions in Soho. In places like Shoreditch, a lot of people are trying to be too cool. Both times we tried to film in Shoreditch we ended up leaving because the atmosphere was so stiff.

One day, we'd been doing some stuff around east London all day and it was very stale. The crew broke for a while, but we had one of the cameras spare. I wanted some energy, something raw, something where people weren't putting on a front, where everyone was too cool for school. So we took the spare camera into Soho where there was a more up-for-it crowd. It was a Friday night and everyone was drunk. They'd lost their inhibitions. I started doing magic there and then, and I truly didn't know what was going to happen.

Randomly, we met a guy just walking down the street in Soho. Finally, we got the reactions we'd been spending hours looking for. After I'd done my identity fraud trick (in which I'd used magic to figure out his bank details and make my bank card transform into one with his name on), I walked off and he started chasing me, thinking I was going to spend his money! The situation was so real that he genuinely believed that I was going to steal his identity. So his real, natural reaction was to chase me down the street to get his card back – which he did. So then I put his phone in a bottle...!

That poor guy, I felt sorry for him. He must have gone home in a totally confused frame of mind.

In some ways, that's my trademark. I'll wait out in the streets for hours to get the best reaction. For the first-ever clip that I posted on YouTube (where I put a playing card through a double-glazed window on an underground train), Dan and I sat on the Central Line for six hours to get it – all ninety seconds of it. It's hard enough to speak to someone on the tube, let alone persuade them to be filmed. But eventually, this guy got on and he agreed to let me show him something amazing. He didn't even seem like he was into it at first and then, all of a sudden, I did the magic and he went crazy – he completely came out of his shell.

We could have sat on the train for an hour and given up, but we waited there for six hours, getting knock-back after knock-back. Most people would have got off that train before we did.

I have that ethic in me when it comes to getting the reaction I want. I might not have the same mindset when it comes to the gym, but when I'm trying to make *Dynamo: Magician Impossible* the very best it can be I'll wait all day and all night to get what I need. I'm passionate about doing what it takes.

I'll never get tired of chasing a good reaction and I'll never get bored of seeing it. I just want to elicit that joy, confusion and astonishment from people when they witness my magic. How many people can say that they go to work and amaze people all day? I don't take for granted how incredible that is.

I love magic because I love watching people's responses when I pull off something incredible. Regardless of what type of magic, where I do it or who I do it on. I'll never get bored of that. Never.

CHAPTER 12

LEAP
OF
FAITH

For the second series of *Dynamo: Magician Impossible*, we had to find lots of new locations to film at to make it feel as fresh and new as the first. LA is the perfect place because you can find totally different scenery in close proximity. Some of my all-time favourite memories have been created there.

If you were to ask me a year ago what the scariest thing I've ever done was, I would have immediately said, 'Walking across the River Thames'. Little did I know what the future had in store; if there's one thing I'm not too fond of, it is heights.

As I stood on the top of the *Los Angeles Times* Building, the bottom looked an awfully long way down. I had decided a few weeks before that I was going to walk down it. Don't ask me why. I wanted to do it. Just me, my trainers and the jumper on my back.

The *LA Times* Building is eighty feet high and situated in the Spring Street area, downtown LA. It was built in 1935 by Gordon Kaufmann, the same guy who designed the Hoover Dam. We wanted to find somewhere that was fairly iconic but not too 'Hollywood'. Downtown LA sounds upmarket, but it's far from the bright lights of Sunset Boulevard, Rodeo Drive and the Hollywood Walk of Fame. The area was once the hub of LA's financial district, but it is now blighted by high unemployment and crime. It reminded me a bit of Delph Hill in that both areas feel cut off from the rest of the world. It's like everyone deserted it in the eighties and at night it feels especially eerie. It's a pretty edgy part of town, but I always like to take my magic where it's least expected. Everyone goes to the Empire State Building but not everyone goes to Harlem. Obviously if you're in Rio you want to see Copacabana beach, but it's also great to experience the City of God neighbourhood.

I wanted to give Spring Street a lasting memory; something that would live with the area forever. Other than that, the building was nice and high and it didn't look too hard for me to sneak in there.

It was around 8 p.m. on a warm evening in LA. I walked confidently inside, strolled up to the elevators and pressed the button. No one stopped me. I stood on the roof for a few minutes to prepare myself. The sun had already set and although it was dark I could just about make out the people below. They looked the size of safety pins. I knew the crew was there somewhere, ready to capture everything, but other than that, I was on my own.

My stomach was churning and I physically couldn't stop my hands and legs from shaking, regardless of how much mind over matter I attempted to employ. I had tried to prepare myself for this, but it was much more frightening than the deathly tides of the River Thames. It was a million times scarier than predicting something live on television or radio. I knew that if my magic didn't work, there was no way I would survive the fall.

The hardest part was mentally preparing myself to go over the edge, and trying to come to terms with the thought of anything going wrong. As I looked down, I tried to compose myself. I had to block out any negative thoughts otherwise I'd never be able to do

if there's one
thing I'm not
fond of, it is
heights

it. The gravity of the situation began to take hold, but I tried to battle my fears head on.

I knew that, if I could pull it off, millions of people would be watching this. I knew that I'd had a great first series and that I needed to have an even better second one. I wanted to test myself; I wanted to push my own physical and mental limitations.

So I simply turned on a switch in my head that would allow me to throw myself off a building.

I went from standing on the top of the building to leaning over the edge, leaning, leaning, leaning, leaning, leaning, leaning, leaning... until I was completely horizontal, and looking at the ground.

Eighty feet in the air and there was only one way to go. When you're afraid of heights everyone says don't look down, but I had no choice!

Under the glare of the street lights, I could see the cars slowing down, the bicycles skidding to a stop, the people looking up at me, their hands covering their mouths in shock.

'What's he doing?'

'Is he going to jump?'

'Should we help him?'

When I first appeared on the roof, people thought I was a suicide jumper. There was a couple watching and when I went over the edge, the woman literally freaked out. Then I started to walk and she freaked out even more. She couldn't believe what she was seeing.

I walked right down the wall, right to the bottom, before stepping off onto the pavement almost like Spider-Man.

I felt every single step of those eighty feet. Walking down the *LA Times* Building, I have never, ever felt closer to death. I can honestly say it's the most terrifying thing I've ever done.

I love that magic gives people the feeling of being young, carefree and open to life's unexpected surprises. When you're a kid you believe you can do anything. It's only as you get older you get cynical and you start to put up barriers. This is why I loved superhero films as a child and what makes me want to recreate the special effects through my magic as an adult.

Why do I do these things? I guess I'm a little bit mental. It's that whole Evel Knievel syndrome. The more you do things successfully, the more you start to feel invincible. And, even if you fail at something, you still learn so much from it.

I believe that passion is the biggest form of motivation. When people ask me why I would walk down a twenty-storey building in LA, I tell them it's because I want to show people that there's more to life than just working nine-to-five. You don't have to follow what everyone else is doing. You can have a mind of your own. You have to go against things and innovate. I like to take the impossible and flip it inside out by using magic.

I think that if I can create it in my head, if I can imagine it, then it must be possible. I think everyone can live their life to their full potential. But it requires work. Everyone has a certain skill set that they are better at than anyone else. Everyone has their own unique selling point; magic just happens to be mine.

♠

If you go to LA thinking Hollywood is all fun and glamour, you'll be quite disappointed. It's just a city. It's a city where people go to work. There are hardly any transport links, meaning the pavements are deserted because everyone drives. The weather is usually warm but because of the pollution it gets really smoggy.

LA is a good city to go to if you are in a position like the one I'm in now. Because I've been there so much and worked with so many people, it really is the City of Dreams for me. If you know people then you will be looked after and you can have the best time of your life in LA. One minute you can be chilling by a hotel pool surrounded by superstars; the next you're averting your eyes as half-naked ladies run about at pool parties. It's a ridiculous city in many ways and I absolutely love it.

Although walking down the *LA Times* Building is top of the list, I've had all types of crazy experiences in Los Angeles. I've hung out with Snoop Dogg and his kids, I've turned paper butterflies into real ones for Natalie Imbruglia and I've performed for Kim

Kardashian, Demi Moore and Ashton Kutcher. I did a card levitation and then I swallowed some string and pulled it out from my stomach. Ashton was pretty freaked out! Kim said to me, 'Are you married?' I didn't take that as an actual proposal!

I have had some of the most surreal moments in LA. In 2009, I flew over to film an advert for adidas alongside Estelle, David Beckham, Run DMC, Katy Perry, The Ting Tings and Missy Elliott to name just a few. Adidas had put me up in the most amazing hotel, the Sunset Marquee, which is just off Sunset Strip. My fellow guests at the hotel included Slipknot and Lil Wayne, and it was by the rooftop pool that I met and made friends with Wayne's manager, Cortez Bryant. Because it was the MTV VMAs weekend, there were the craziest parties every night and my feet barely touched the ground as I went from one glamorous party to the next.

One of the best was at a hotel called the Chateau Marmont. It's a faux-French castle just off Sunset Boulevard that is notorious for its wild parties. Everyone from Leonardo DiCaprio to John Lennon has stayed there. The actor John Belushi died in one of the bungalows after a drug overdose. Jim Morrison from The Doors nearly broke his back after dangling from a drainpipe and falling onto a shed (as you do). Lindsay Lohan occasionally moves in and lives there for a few months, causing all kinds of havoc. It's the most rock and roll hotel I've ever been to.

On this particular evening, Nellee Hooper was throwing a party. If you don't know who Nellee is, well, he's a legend. This is the guy who has produced hits for Soul II Soul, Massive Attack, Madonna, No Doubt, U2, Björk... the list goes on and on.

Nellee was hosting an event for a new company that he had just set up, called Talent House. It was basically about taking British talent out to America and introducing them to the right people.

This event was unreal: there were only fifty people in attendance and they were all Hollywood elite. You had everyone from Paris and Nicky Hilton, Benji and Joel Madden from Good Charlotte, Russell Simmons, Bow Wow, Jermaine Dupri, T.I., Sacha Baron Cohen and his wife Isla Fisher. I had been invited along to entertain them with my magic.

One person I met there was Anthony Kiedis from the Red Hot Chili Peppers. We just fell into conversation when I received a message on my phone from my sister. It was a picture of my brand-new niece, Ruby.

Anthony leaned over and smiled, 'Ahh, who's the kid?' I told him she was my niece. 'Oh, I love kids, you've got to see pictures of mine,' he said, pulling out his phone. We spent the next twenty minutes looking at photos of his children and having this full-on conversation about our upbringings.

My friends will always ask me, 'Oh, what was so-and-so famous person like?' and it's really hard to say. Most famous people you meet, you rock up, do some magic, they say 'cool' and off you go. It's only the very few, like Ian Brown or De La Soul, that I make proper friends with. With most celebrities, they don't have time to hold a conversation or you end up chatting about industry stuff. Whereas with Anthony Kiedis, we had an impromptu but genuine, natural conversation about life.

He was the coolest guy I've ever spoken to, ever. I've chatted with a lot of cool people, but he was something else.

The next day, I went to film the adidas advert. The concept was that of a 'House Party' and we shot it at the Warner Brothers studio in the Chevy Chase house from the National Lampoon films. It's an iconic location and as a movie fan, it was great to get to see it in the flesh. The ad was jam-packed with stars, from David Beckham to Estelle, to the designer Jeremy Scott,

Run DMC, Russell Simmons, Young Jeezy and Missy Elliott. The crew filmed as we danced, threw cake around, jumped on beanbags – but of course the real party happened when the cameras weren't rolling.

My dressing room was next to Missy Elliott and Estelle and so we spent lots of time together, hanging out and listening to music. I ended up chilling with Russell Simmons outside the house, while Run from Run DMC chatted to Method Man and Redman, who were running around causing mayhem in their typical style!

I remember sitting with Missy on the fountain that can be seen in the opening titles of *Friends*, talking to her about the magic that I do and the music that she makes. It was so surreal.

Honestly, there are only certain times I can really say this, but 'only in LA'. What a city.

♠

I couldn't mention LA and not talk about my boys. I didn't realise it when we started filming, but in some ways, *Dynamo: Magician Impossible* is like magic's version of *Entourage*. Or *Dynamo: Magician Impossible* is like *Entourage* with magic.

The show is set in LA and features an actor and his best mates from Brooklyn having the time of their lives as they navigate their way through new-found fame and fortune.

Like the TV series' main character, Vince, I roll everywhere with my boys. They have been there for me throughout everything – the ups and the downs, the highs and the lows. I couldn't make a programme about me without showing the guys who make up such a huge part of my life. With the second series in particular, I think people really got to see another side of me through my friends' presence in the show.

There are quite a few people who make up my 'entourage'.
I couldn't possibly namecheck everyone in this book, so apologies
to those not mentioned here.

Firstly, there are my boys from Bradford. There are the guys who
I grew up with and who are my friends for life. Without their
help, support and encouragement, I'd never have made the
move to London and pursued my career. These guys are my core
group of friends who have been with me pretty much every step
of the way.

Marcus and I go way, way back. I was friends with his little
brother, who I knew from the MAPA youth club on Delph Hill. I
didn't hang out with Marcus too much, but one time I was in
town and his brother had to go to work, so we ended up chilling
out for the day.

It was someone's birthday and Marcus asked, 'Do you want to go
to the party and do some magic?' I said, 'Yeah, cool.' We were
already in the town centre and because I lived in Delph Hill,
which was ages away on the bus, he just said, 'We'll go to mine
across the street first and you can borrow some of my clothes.'
So, we went to his house and partied that night and then we

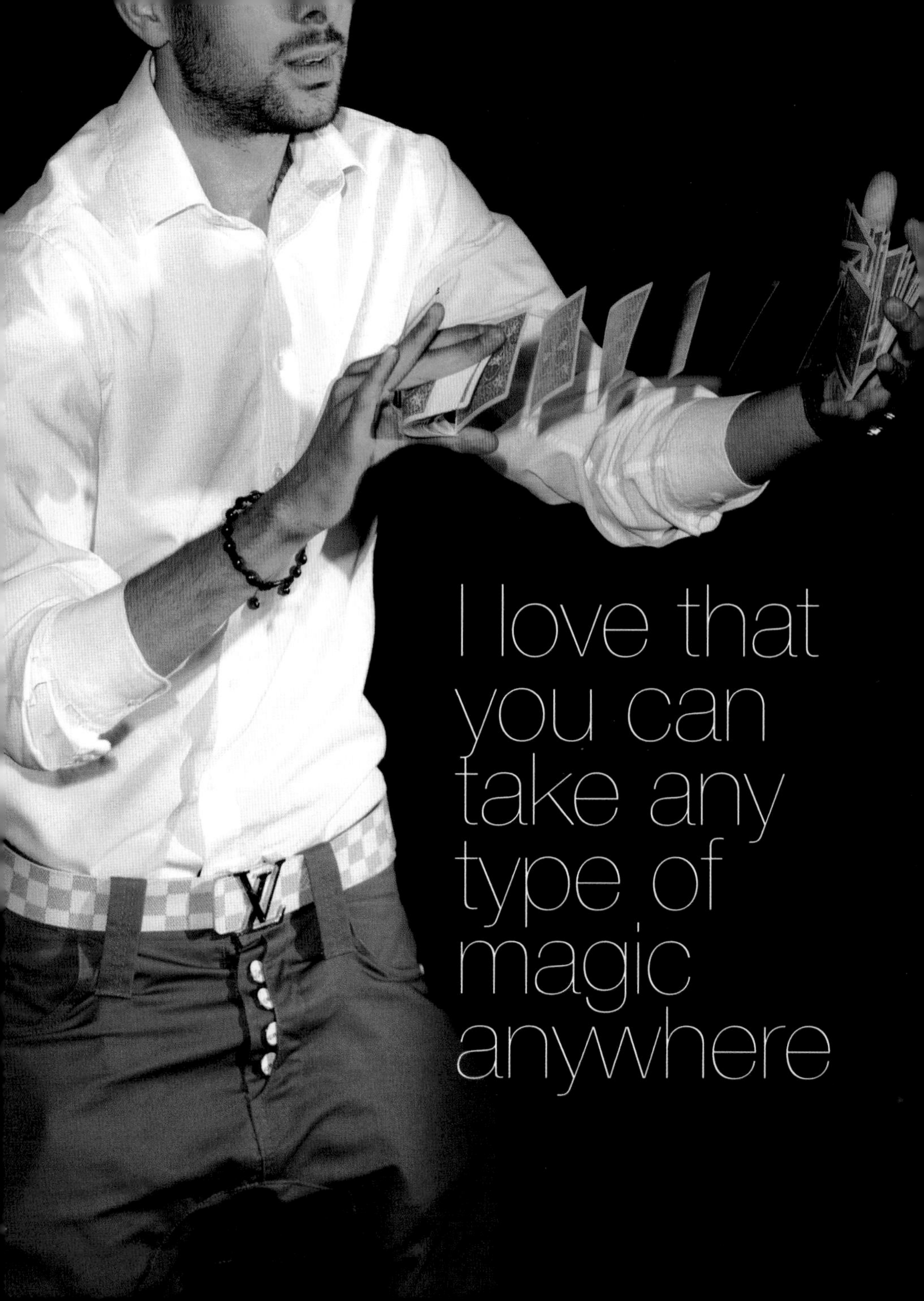

I love that
you can
take any
type of
magic
anywhere

Performing a suspension on a park bench in Rio.

Not everything I do is for the faint-hearted.

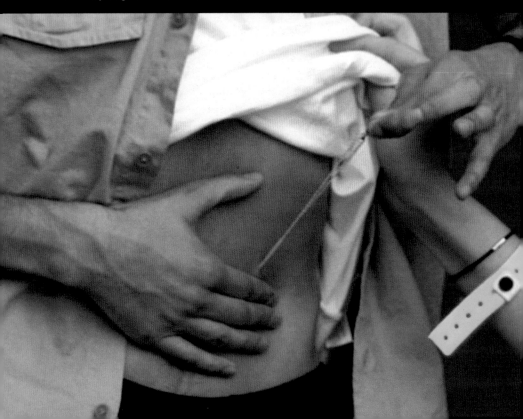

Flying over the crowd to make my way out of a club.

Hands on fire. Don't try this at home!

this was the
moment I'd
been building
up to my
whole life

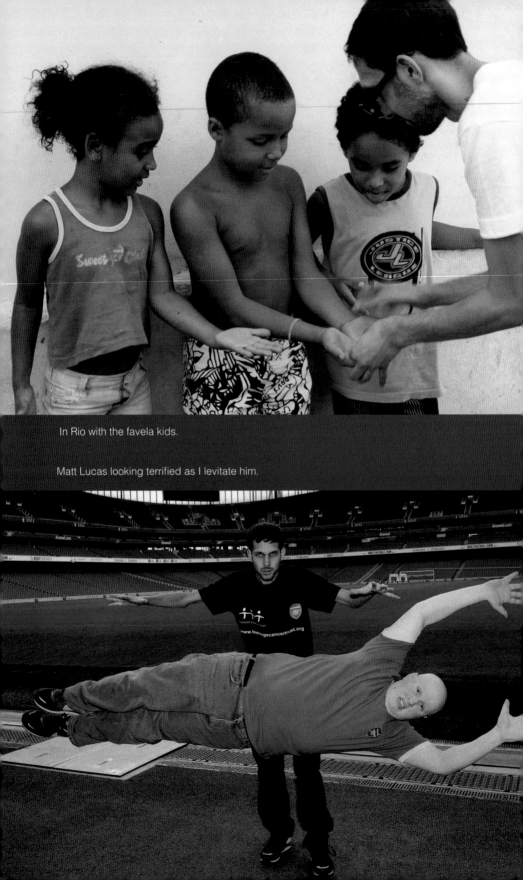

In Rio with the favela kids.

Matt Lucas looking terrified as I levitate him.

Levitating myself at Christ the Redeemer.

Another phone, another bottle.

Phillip Schofield trying his hardest to lift me after I'd taken his strength away.

literally saw each other every day after that for three months straight. Although he still lives in Bradford and we can't meet up daily now, he's my best friend. Marcus is one of those guys who never had a lot, he's never had it easy, but he always sees the positive side of things. He's always smiling and never unhappy. He's a really positive influence on me because if I do get down, I think of Marcus and get myself together.

Alex's real name in Aloizy – but Alex is a lot easier to say. He used to drive around in a Citroën Saxo and was always there for me if I needed him. He's always up for a laugh. He has a wife and kids now and is working as a joiner in Bradford.

Johnny was the kid who was a bit richer than the rest of us. He lived in an amazing house next to my school, Wyke Manor. Everyone always used to go, 'Whose house is that?' He didn't attend our school, but the first time I met Johnny he walked through the school with a couple of his friends and one of them had a fight with some guy. His mate just rolled in, decked the guy, and walked back out again. Everyone was like, 'Who *was* that guy?' He and his friends were skateboarders, so when I went to a skate park I ended up skateboarding with them. We just started to hang out from there. Johnny now works as a mentor at a school for kids who have been expelled from other schools.

Bolaji was always the quiet one of the group and also one of the most hardworking. He's always gone out of his way to stay in touch. He's studying to be a pilot. If I ever get to the stage where I can have a private jet – Belaji, you've got to be my pilot!

Dennis is from the neighbouring town of Huddersfield. It was Dennis who taught me to dance at MAPA. Without him I might not have found my signature shuffle. He also did the choreography for *Concrete Playground* and my stage show. He continues to work with me today.

Obviously, since I've moved to London I've met a lot of people in my personal and professional life. They've been so supportive and made the transition from Bradford to London so much easier. Asif, Titanya, Stef, Chris, Luti, Alfie, Gilera, Sean, Tony, Gary, Darren, Maria, Paula, Hattie, Daisy... are just a few. Not forgetting my production and camera crew. Don't worry, guys, I consider you friends as well as colleagues!

There's one other person from London who has become one of my best friends and biggest supporter – my manager Dan.

Behind every successful entertainer is a strong team. You can't achieve much if you don't have people around you who you can trust. Other than Gramps, I owe a lot of my success to Dan, who has been my manager since 2003. That's a long time in anyone's book, but it's even longer when you consider that we've only really been properly successful for the last two years. Before that we were doing all right, but it's been a long, hard struggle to reach the point I'm at now. And Dan has been with me for most of that journey.

Without good management, then you can be lost as an artist. You need someone who you can trust to help you navigate your way through not only the pitfalls of business, but also things like arranging to pick you up at 3 a.m., covering for you when you're sick and making sure you get a break and something to eat when you've been working for twelve hours solid. It's the same in real life as it is in business. You need to have a solid team of supportive people, who care about you and will be there through your bad times as well as your successes. Without good friends, you're nothing.

It hasn't always been easy. This crazy journey I've been on has tested our friendship at times, but we're family now. He's like my mouth and ears. I'm not really that great when it comes to discussing the ins and outs of business. I like to go in, wow people and then let Dan get us the best deal possible. He understands me and my magical mind better than anyone and he understands what I'm trying to achieve.

He's been a mentor, a brother, a friend and a manager. In some ways, some of the biggest tests we've had have been over the last two years and together we've both adjusted to the increasing pressure. There's a lot more riding on everything now and we both have to ensure that we don't make mistakes.

I want to sustain my career. I want to show people that I'm not a one-trick pony. I want to keep the magic alive. I want to leave a legacy and that's what I'm working towards. If I thought I could do all that on my own, I'd be a fool. But thankfully I have Dan.

CHAPTER 13

FLYING HIGH IN THE FAVELAS

The taxi driver didn't speak much English. 'Corcovado,' he muttered, a few minutes after pulling out of Rio de Janeiro-Galeão International Airport, nodding towards the imposing statue of Christ the Redeemer that silently watches over the city. 'Samba,' he continued as we passed a school of music housing students of one of Brazil's most enduring musical creations. 'Favela,' came last, but certainly not least, as he gestured towards the hillside slums that contain around 20 per cent of Rio's six-million-strong populace. That's around 1.2 million people. Rio's thousand-odd favelas have become as synonymous with the country as Pelé, palm trees, waxing and Barry Manilow's 'Copacabana'.

He may have been a man of few words, but my cabbie had a point: religion, music and poverty could, to the casual observer, pretty much sum up Rio de Janeiro. Yet to reduce the South American city to a mere three words does a huge disservice to this utterly magical place. The city's extraordinary situation between sparkling sea and densely forested mountains, its vibrancy and its outstanding natural beauty, led UNESCO to declare Rio a World Heritage Site.

It's a twelve-hour flight from the UK to Brazil and getting there is pretty exhausting. I left London at night-time and landed a day later as dawn broke over Rio. Viewing the city for the first time, soaked in an incredible red mist, my jet lag instantly disappeared.

Rio is such a visual experience – it's a total assault on your senses. You have the beaches, the ocean, Sugar Loaf Mountain, the Tijuca Forest that surrounds the imposing statue of Christ the Redeemer – and the city itself, which is a sprawling mass of churches, skyscrapers, graffiti, winding streets, motorbikes, cars, rollerbladers and food stalls selling aromatic street food. It's noisy, hot and beautiful. With its palm trees, hot, white sands and buff bodies squeezed into the smallest of swimsuits, the beaches are postcard perfect. And the women... Well, let's say I've never seen so many gorgeous people in one city in my whole life.

It was the perfect place to film for my second series we wanted everything to be bigger and better than what we'd done so far. Rio gave me all the inspiration I needed to create some of the most 'magical' moments in my career.

I'd been looking forward to going to Rio so much, not only because I'd never been there before, but also because it was not long after Gramps had sadly passed away on 29 February 2012. I needed something to reignite me; something to distract me from my heartache. I fell out of love with magic for a while. When Gramps died, the magic seemed to die with him. I just couldn't be bothered and I had no motivation to do anything. Things got so overwhelming that I wanted to make myself disappear – but this time forever. I hoped that by going to Rio, where no one knew me, no one had heard of me, and no one knew what I did, I would rediscover my love of magic.

I wasn't disappointed. Rio was everything I had hoped it would be, and more.

You can watch *City of God* as many times as you like before you arrive in Rio, but as powerful a film as it may be, 38mm of celluloid doesn't do justice to the contradictions of poverty, wealth, corruption and opportunity that exist within the mountain-framed metropolis. The city is rich in music, food, art and theatre. Sadly, until recently, the biggest talking point about Rio was its endemic violence. Poor policing, exacerbated by low wages, ingrained state corruption, entrenched racism and a proliferation of drugs and firearms made Rio one of the most violent cities in the world. There are, on average, 1.9 murders per 100,000 people in London each year, compared to 37 murders per 100,000 people in Rio. There are three times as many people killed, on average, by the police in Rio each year, than are killed by police annually in the whole of the United States.

Yet, with the World Cup arriving in 2014 and the Olympics in 2016, it's a city that is being cleaned up. Brazil's property prices are among the fastest rising in the world, and the country's economic development is bucking European and American trends by booming, not recessing. It's a nation on the up; a rising force. I couldn't wait to explore it for myself. The city is reaching new heights and I wanted to do exactly the same!

♠

To get acclimatised, I walked around a lot during the first few days, soaking up the atmosphere of the city. My magic is always organic and I like to freestyle and adjust to my surroundings. I rarely plan what I'm going to do beforehand, especially with close-up magic.

Rio gave me all the inspiration I needed

Because most of the people there speak little or no English and my Portuguese is, well, non-existent, I really had to rely on magic to break the language barrier. As I've found throughout the world, I don't need to speak the local dialect; magic always does the talking for me.

After spending a bit of time seeing what the city was about, one thing that became immediately apparent was that everywhere you go you see guys selling fresh coconuts. They chop off the top with a machete and stick a straw inside. So I devised a piece of magic based around them. I would ask one of the tourists or locals to name a drink and then ask them to choose a fresh coconut from the guy selling them. They'd order a Coke or an orange juice – someone even said coffee – and the guy would cut their coconut of choice open, then they would pour out the liquid inside…only it would turn out that it wasn't coconut milk – it would be whatever drink they had requested. I do something similar in the UK with bottles of Coke and Fanta. In some ways, that piece of magic harks back to what Gramps showed me with the red and green matches.

Whether I switch drinks in Covent Garden or on Copacabana beach, using bottles or coconuts, it always baffles people. It's all about using everyday things to create the unexpected. Making the familiar unfamiliar is the best way to surprise people. They go from feeling at ease to completely shocked. And somewhere in between that quick switch of emotions is where magic lies.

Night-time in Rio is when the city comes alive, so I figured a stroll along Copacabana's iconic boardwalk would be a good start. Rio's street culture is great – everywhere you look, something is going on. Some of the things I saw literally made me stop in my tracks. There were old men doing mind-blowing footwork with footballs and on the sand I saw groups of people practising capoeira – a Brazilian martial art that combines dance and

music. Watching the incredibly controlled yet fluid inventiveness made me feel like a kid again. I was mesmerised and lost in the magic of the moment. With this image in mind, I decided to do my own version of capoeira. I found a bench beside the seafront and with just one arm for balance I did a half-levitation, inspired by the moves I had seen the capoeira dancers perform.

As dusk falls in Rio, local kids rush to the popcorn stalls, which are everywhere. They are like the Brazilian equivalent of our ice-cream vans, except they sell popcorn. I decided to set up my own business. But rather than using a popcorn machine, I just used my hands. Initially, I made the kernels pop inside a glass much to the delight of the crowd of kids who had gathered. Then, with the heat from my palms, I rubbed my hands together and piles of popcorn sprang out. The kids went nuts. Some of the best reactions I've ever had have been in Rio.

I was also in Rio for with the infamous Carnival. During those five days some two million people descend onto the streets for the world's biggest street party. It's incredible to see so many people coming together to celebrate life. The sheer spectacle of Carnival has the power to break down all cultural barriers – the loud music, extravagantly decorated floats, the animated dancing and outrageous costumes can be understood in any language.

As I wandered further into the city, Carnival was in full flow, so I decided to bring a little bit more magic to the festival. Deep in the thick of the dancers, floats and tourists, I spotted a guy selling maracas, a classic South American percussion instrument. I asked a woman to draw something on a coin – she chose a heart. Then, I took her to the maracas seller and asked her to pick one; she did and I shook it to demonstrate that there was only the standard rice inside. I continued to shake it and the more I shook the less noise it made, until there was only one noise left.

It sounded suspiciously like the rattling of a coin. I asked the seller to smash the instrument with his foot and all that was left inside was the coin. I picked it up and gave her back her heart.

♠

Once we'd done the beaches and the Carnival, I wanted to go to where the action was. People say that the real heartbeat of Rio is found in the favelas, yet they're a part of Rio that most visitors avoid.

Some of the favelas are flat and warren-like, a riddle of dusty corridors that wind over several square miles. Most of them, though, sprawl up Rio's various mountains, boasting the best views in the city. As the sun sets on Ipanema beach, you can look up to the favelas and see the mountains light up. It's really stunning. I'm not exaggerating when I say Rio is one of the most invigorating, exhilarating, interesting places I've ever visited.

I went to the outskirts of a couple of favelas – including Cidade de Deus, which is also known as the City of God – and immediately felt I wasn't welcome. You could sense the danger around you and see the distrust on people's faces. I might have been there to entertain with my magic, but the locals were unsure and didn't want me or my camera crew there. It's a shame. I'm positive that had I had the chance to do even one piece of magic then we might have had a different reception. But you have to realise when you're not welcome and carefully back away. When you're a stranger to somewhere, you have to respect the local people's codes and learn to pick up on the nuances of body language and the atmosphere. Most importantly, you have to accept when you need to get the hell out!

The Chapéu Mangueira favela, though, was comparatively safe. It's set on the borders of Copacabana and Ipanema, overlooking the beaches and Christ the Redeemer, and it has the most stunning views. If you wanted an apartment with the best vista of Rio, Chapéu Mangueira is where you'd want it to be located.

Although Chapéu Mangueira is considered safe, you can't just walk into a favela alone and you need to keep your wits about you. We met a guy called Tiago who agreed to be our guide. His home was at the top of the favela and he invited us over for lunch with his mum.

A couple of guys tried to test us while we were there, but generally it was one of the most warm and welcoming places I've ever visited and we were able to stay through the night. That said, while we were having lunch at Tiago's, I heard a loud bang. 'What was that?' I asked him. 'Football match,' he replied, as another bang echoed across the favela. 'Hmm, doesn't sound like the kind of football I play,' I said. Who knows what those bangs were, but they certainly didn't sound football-based to my ears. There was a dangerous side to the favela, but for me it was just incredible; it was full of magical experiences.

There's so much more to learn by visiting those communities. Although I was warned of the dangers, I knew this was where I needed to show people my magic. It was quite risky filming up there, but it was important to me to show both sides of Rio and not to dwell on the negative aspects of it.

The kids in the favela told me that it's actually a lot safer for them in their neighbourhood than it is on the 'tarmac', which is what they call the beaches down below. It's safer because most of the crime happens down there and not in the favela itself, unless you're directly involved in drug dealing. A lot of these kids go down to hustle the tourists, so that's when you might have problems. There they might see someone from a rival favela, hustle the wrong person or get pulled over by the police.

Brazil is a notoriously corrupt country. It's known that in the past drug gangs have been supported by the police. The police seem to be a law unto themselves and are probably the most dangerous gang in Brazil. For the favela kids, the police are their biggest enemy and their greatest fear.

Although violence is inevitable, normal life continues as it would anywhere. Loud music pumps out of the concrete shacks, corrugated iron structures that serve loosely as shops sell sweets, acai, beer and biscuits and hundreds of kites flitter on the skyline. The Brazilians have a real thing for kites – when you're in the favela, everywhere you look there are different coloured flags skipping in the sky. It's really beautiful. There's some incredible graffiti, really intricately painted murals that cover almost every available inch of wall. Telephone cable and wires hang everywhere. I don't know what happens if your electricity goes off because I don't know how they'd ever unravel that mess of wire. Everywhere you look you see random things like some guy carrying a fridge, chickens in cages and washing hanging up anywhere a bit of sun can get through to dry the clothes.

People are all around, talking, laughing, gossiping and hanging out. It felt like such a stark contrast to the estates I had grown up in. In Delph Hill, everyone is hidden away and no one really talks to each other. There's a lot of fear and, after dark, people hide away in their homes to avoid any drama that might be happening on the streets. Any community spirit that did exist seems to have long gone. In contrast, the favelas of Rio are always alive. You get Sky TV up there, so people are gathered around televisions, watching the football. The kids are out playing; people are sat out on their steps, talking, arguing, laughing while the TV blares in the background. Groups of friends sit around tables eating food and drinking 'cerveja' (beer). They have these huge parties – Baile Funks – where they basically rave all night to the loudest, bassiest music you've ever heard.

Every step leads you to another magical site. Could Rio be the home of magic? I think it could be!

The thing that warmed my heart most was how the children followed me everywhere. I was like the Pied Piper of the favela! It was quite tough going, physically, because the favelas are carved into the mountainside. To get up into Mangueira, you find a path near the beach and then you have the choice of taking a narrow winding road up via motorbike (my choice!); an elevator-like contraption that drags you upwards; or there's a steep staircase that cuts right up through the middle of the favela. If you consider the elevator is 64 metres high (the equivalent of a twenty-three-storey building) then you won't blame me for avoiding the stairs. Even with that steep hill, the kids would run after me on the motorbike taxi, laughing and asking for more magic. They followed me everywhere.

In the favela, I used whatever I could find for my magic. The paths were littered with random, weird objects, old junk and discarded toys. Also, as the locals speak very little English, I had to break the language barrier visually. At one point, I found a piece of old wire on the floor. I asked this woman her name and she said, 'Juliana'. In the blink of an eye, I bent the wire into her name. She couldn't believe it.

What I loved most was the sense of the unexpected. Once, we were filming late at night. I was performing some magic that involved a bingo game. The game was taking place down a dark alleyway, so it all looked quite sinister. There was an eerie orange glow from the street lamps and shadows lurking everywhere. Suddenly, one of the shutters opened up on one of

the shacks to the left of us. This very pale face poked out, and then another, and then another. It turned out to be a young woman from Reading whose mum and dad were there to visit her. We spoke briefly to the woman who told us she had come to Rio to teach favela kids English and had ended up moving in.

It was so bizarre and the last thing you'd ever expect to see. You build up a picture of a place, but those images are always inaccurate. It's like being in Jamaica; you don't hear reggae coming over the hills, you hear Michael Bolton and Celine Dion! It's really funny – how you expect things to be and how things actually are can be very different. The element of surprise is sacred to me. I love that life is full of those moments.

I was in Rio for eleven days and on my final day, I decided to visit Christ the Redeemer. I'd always wanted to do a levitation at a world-renowned landmark. I'd levitated Lindsay Lohan in Singapore, I'd levitated Matt Lucas at the Emirates Stadium, so now I wanted to levitate myself at Christ the Redeemer.

To get to the top you take a tram that drags you up the steep hillside. Then you walk up a lot of stairs. Finally, you go up some more stairs! It's so high that it takes about an hour to reach the peak. On the way up, a thick mist started to roll in. I had no idea if I'd even be able to see the city when I levitated. Would the weather be against me, or would the mist disperse and make the levitation as magical as I anticipated it would be?

I'd imagined the Redeemer to be a place of still, silent tranquility. The revered statue is so tremendous and so isolated that I assumed it would be like visiting a church.

I was wrong. As I reached the peak, the mist finally lifting, I was greeted by both incredible views and the sight of hundreds of tourists taking pictures of the statue.

I asked a woman if she'd take a picture of me in front of the Redeemer. She agreed and I climbed the stairs, coming to a stop near the top. I took a deep breath and then slowly, with my arms outstretched, I started to rise. My frame echoing the almighty sculpture behind me.

Before long, I was hovering above the crowd as they all looked up at me in amazement. The noise that had greeted me when I first got there dissipated and the crowd stood in silence as I rose before Christ.

I got goosebumps all over my skin as I looked down at the people watching and the panoramic view behind. It was utterly awe-inspiring. There was the ocean spreading out as far as the eye could see, surrounded by white sandy beaches and the city, fizzing and sparkling below. People had come to take pictures of the statue, but as well as the iconic 365-tonne sculpture, they found me, floating in the sky. It was a risky thing to portray something with a religious connotation – similar to the River Thames walk – but that's not intentional. And it wasn't intended to offend people. These types of things appear in the Bible because they are miracles. They shouldn't happen. And my drive comes from trying to make the impossible possible.

That moment in time created an everlasting image in my mind of this amazing city. It's something I'll take away and cherish for the rest of my life.

Like I said earlier, though, it's not about the scale – it's all about the element of surprise and amazement. Whether it's a huge death-defying stunt, a prediction or close-up magic on the street, the philosophies and the principles are the same. It doesn't matter if I'm levitating above Christ the Redeemer or doing something crazy with a deck of cards in the favelas, I always want to elicit the same response from my magic.

Putting a phone inside a bottle, to me, is as impressive as levitating myself in front of Christ the Redeemer in Brazil. That's how I see it, anyway.

Although I've told you about the different categories of magic, I really break it down into just two types: physical and mental. The physical can range from something small, like bending my finger in weird ways, to walking across the Thames. They're both still physical pieces of magic. The mental magic that I do can consist of anything from a prediction in front of a live audience to something like reading Snoop's mind over Twitter.

Walking across the River Thames is as big and as magical as bringing butterflies to life in a hotel. But you can make the scale of smaller magic 'bigger' by changing how and where you do it. I can do card magic to a celebrity and it's bigger because it's a celebrity. I could walk across a swimming pool, but it's bigger when it's the River Thames. I could change a picture, but because it's Tinie Tempah's album cover rather than my nan's crossword puzzle, the scale seems bigger. And because the scale is bigger, the perception of what I've done is therefore bigger. But they're all the same to me and I like to think that all my magic causes the same powerful reaction in the spectator too. It's just the bigger things seem to stick in people's memories longer.

As the years have gone by, my determination to push the boundaries of what I do has grown. Every idea I come up with now, I start with something small and then my ambition kicks in. No matter what the thing is, I want to make it as big as it can possibly be. It's like I have some kind of switch in me because there's nothing I won't attempt, no matter how scary.

Sometimes, with magic, it can come down to luck and coincidence. But then, luck is often misconstrued because, to me, luck is when the preparation meets the opportunity. I could find heaps of great opportunities all the time, but if I haven't worked on my skills and I don't know how to handle that opportunity, then it's going to be wasted.

For a long time I used to perform something and not remember it afterwards. It was a blur, because adrenalin took over. The River Thames walk is where I finally started to become more conscious of what was going on. I began to feel the adrenalin and almost learn how to control it. I don't remember the first few steps of walking across the Thames. But as I got further out, I began to feel my surroundings, I started to hear the people. Before that day I wouldn't really notice – I was in the zone.

Series two and three took me to so many new and exciting places. I feel so fortunate. It's often the cases that places where there is extreme poverty are also places of incredible creativity. I saw that in Rio and there are examples throughout the whole history of film, music and art where the greatest work has emerged from places of hardship – Al Pacino was homeless when he first started out and had to sleep in a theatre!

A few years ago, I went to a centre for kids from my home town who had been expelled from school. They had been sent to a PRU (Pupil Referral Unit) and they were so rowdy. Before I did my first piece of magic, it was basically chaos; they were shouting, swearing and running around. Suddenly, I pulled a Polo mint out of my neck and it went very, very quiet. You could hear a pin drop. They were transfixed. I like that my magic can do that – break barriers and change a person's frame of mind. The kids at the PRU were the same as the kids in Rio; completely mesmerised while they watched and then full of noise, laughter and astonishment when I finished. It was a similar scene when I intervened with a group of rival fans at a football match between Bradford City and Leeds United several years ago. Just as things threatened to turn nasty, I pulled out a deck of cards. For a moment you had the two groups of opposing fans laughing together; their hostilities temporarily forgotten. I'm not saying magic can heal the world, but it definitely made it a better place for me and the people I performed to that day.

I try to look at the extremes of my life – where I've come from and where I'm going – to learn something. Otherwise, what's the point? I really believe you have to question things to improve every aspect of who you are. Because the first series of *Dynamo: Magician Impossible* did so well, I could have made a second series full of superstars and Lamborghinis. But that didn't interest me. I've always been about taking my magic to everyday people in everyday situations. Series two and three were different.

The desire to go to places that other people would avoid goes back to my *Concrete Playground* DVD, which I made after *Underground Magic* in 2006. When we shot that, we went to two rival estates in Birmingham: Lozells and Ladywood. I don't know how it is now, but back then they were at war with each other. It was really quite serious. We got in there through a friend of ours and we went specifically to show another side these notorious estates.

If you watch *Concrete Playground*, the reactions were a joy. These kids were brilliant – the fact we had bothered to go there and do something for them was really appreciated. We also got to hear what they were up to and it turned out there were some amazing rappers, singers and producers in that part of Birmingham. So much talent goes unseen because there's no outlet for it. By using footage of these brilliant, warm, hilarious kids and talented teenagers we took away that hard, scary image that people assume they will find in deprived areas.

With *Dynamo: Magician Impossible*, I wanted to go to Rio to show the other side of the favelas, rather than the stereotypical images we are often fed. If I was in New York, I'd rather take my camera to Harlem's Rucker Park and show the basketball players some tricks instead of hanging out in a ritzy uptown restaurant. Even when I walked down a building in LA, I chose to do it far away from Hollywood. Downtown LA is a pretty rough place. I want to take my magic to people who aren't ordinarily exposed to the wonders of life on a daily basis. I'll never forget the feeling Gramps conjured up inside me when he magically changed the length of those laces. I've never let go of it and want everyone else to feel it too. It doesn't equate to anything else.

I hope that by taking magic to people from all walks of life I can show that really we're all the same. That, to me, is what's so interesting – revealing that you can meet incredibly welcoming, hospitable people in places we assume will be hostile. Like in

Rio, it is sometimes difficult because people can be very wary and distrusting of strangers, but I try where I can. I like to take my magic to places that most performers don't bother to go to. I wanted to give people something for nothing; especially to people who are rich in spirit.

Magic uncovers people's personalities. We all put up a front, but magic breaks through those barriers. It takes us to the common ground that everyone shares, to the thing that connects us all together. Everyone wants to be happy, to laugh, to be amazed. My favourite thing about magic is the honesty it brings out in people; when we see something that amazes us, our natural, pure emotion comes out. You don't see that much these days.

CHAPTER 14

REALITY IS WHAT YOU MAKE IT

'What's going on here, G – has someone been murdered or something?' Gilera slowed the car down as we looked at the eight police officers and five security officers trying, unsuccessfully, to hold back the crowds of people.

'Something doesn't add up. There are thousands of people here, what's going on?' murmured G, stopping the car altogether.

Dan had told me that I had a show at 3 p.m. at Whitehaven Festival. I would be performing some magic for people in the VIP area. I thought it would be some kind of glorified village fete. The Red Arrows were doing a display, Martin from *Coronation Street* (who now makes cheese) had a stall and the Bay City Rollers were closing the night with a headline set. I wasn't even booked on the main stage; I'd be wandering around doing my magic among the festival-goers.

Then I got there, and 12,000 people swarmed to see me.

It's really hard for me to consider myself famous. I've had to accept that it's a part of my life now, but fame just isn't a word I associate with myself. I do magic. I don't do fame.

When the organisers announced that I would be doing a walk-through around the town, every single one of the 12,000 festival attendees rushed over to the main street. Obviously, they didn't have the resources to cope with such huge numbers. We quickly parked up and the organisers hastily reorganised a performance in the nearby arena.

Not long before Whitehaven, I innocently tweeted that I'd be doing an appearance at Westfield Stratford City in London. That was the first time I really saw a response from 'fans'. I was appearing at store opening for adidas. When we got there, I saw a huge queue had formed outside the store, meaning only a small percentage of the people gathered would get in. They'd let ten people in at a time and so I moved as quickly as I could so I could see as many people as possible. One girl was so nervous when she met me that she was physically shaking.

All I could hear from outside were people chanting: 'Dynamo! Dynamo! Dynamo!' I decided to leave the store so I could say 'hi' to as many people as possible. A couple of the store security guards escorted us as I started to sign autographs. But then, all of a sudden, it got really mental. The crowd began jostling around and we were worried that people would get hurt because everyone was pushing and shoving each other. It was mad. Before I knew it another three security guys were by my side, leading me down the escalators. Behind me, I could see everyone running for the stairs, crowding around the balconies and ahead of us there was a large group gathering at the bottom of the escalators. I couldn't believe that people were doing this because of me. Eventually, we had to get a police escort to get us out of the shopping centre and into the car park. I think the security guys were as surprised as us – no one had expected a reaction like that.

I do find it really weird. I understand people get excited to meet musicians and actors – I certainly did when I first started coming to London and I'd meet people I admired like the rapper Wiley. 'Oh my God, Wiley, it's you, you're so sick. Can I show you some of my magic?' Who doesn't get excited to meet someone they respect and admire? But when you have thousands of people screaming and asking for autographs and near enough knocking each other over to get a look at me, it's very overwhelming.

My life has definitely changed. I'll never forget the day *Dynamo: Magician Impossible* aired and we had twelve times the number of viewers that the channel normally gets. We'd broken all records on Watch. I was at a cash point and I had £7 in my bank account. I couldn't even get a tenner out. I had the biggest show on Watch and no money. But a week later, I went from having £7 to more money than I'd had in my account, ever. Obviously, now things are a bit different and I don't have to worry as much about money as I used to. But fame doesn't always equate to vast riches – at least not straight away.

I am slowly starting to see a bit of money, so I'm trying to be wise with it. We've all heard about the stars that went bankrupt because they were stupid with their cash. I'm interested in making lifelong investments in things that are close to me.

One thing that magic has given me is an appreciation for other art forms. I'm certainly a lot more cultured than I used to be, because magic has given me access to places and people I might never have seen or met. When I've performed in palaces and museums, I've been exposed to the most magnificent art, artefacts and architecture.

I've got a Banksy which is one of twenty-five. I'm trying to invest in things that are a moment in time. I do like fast cars and some of the other finer things in life, but now I'm trying to spend the money I have wisely.

S ometimes I wonder if my life has all been an illusion, but if there's one thing I've learnt, it's that reality is only what you make it.

It's so crazy how things can change so quickly. Even though it's taken twelve years of building towards this moment, it feels like the switch happened overnight. And because I had a whole decade of ups and downs, I feel like I've handled it better. There's a reason that it took so long. And now, I certainly appreciate everything a lot more because I had to wait.

Dynamo: Magician Impossible is now broadcast in 192 countries across the world. It's on the Discovery Channel in South Africa and I have so many fans there now. Even in America, I get people recognising me. I used to film a lot of my close-up scenes in Covent Garden, but I can't do that now because hundreds of people stop to watch and it gets out of control.

I think over time that a bit of a separation between the private and the public me has developed. Earlier on there wasn't – I was just me, and you'd call me D, Dynamo, Steve, whatever. Now, though, there has to be a separation because Dynamo is a much bigger entity.

'Dynamo' is the public me now, whereas 'Steven' still represents my personal life. My girlfriend is one of the few people who actually call me by my real name. It's been important for me to make a distinction between the two as it helps me keep things in perspective.

There aren't too many differences between Dynamo and Steven. Maybe Dynamo is slightly more confident and more self-assured in his abilities. Whereas me, Steven, I'm still learning how to deal with fame, with my woman and business, and all the different things that are changing around me. Dynamo hangs out in the coolest clubs and bars all over the world, but Steven likes to stay in with his mates and watch a movie.

I look back at those days hiding away in my room

I've spent a long time putting my life into magic to get myself where I am. Along the way I have created an online family of followers; people who love my work and support me no matter what, which still surprises me. It's not like I have the best interpersonal skills. I wasn't allowed to play out much, because of the drug dealers on my estate. And it's not as though I was in my house playing with friends or anything – I was just in my bedroom by myself practising with my cards.

I suppose I've had to educate myself, because even at school I was misunderstood. Most people would call me a 'geek' or a 'loser', but I just call it 'being misunderstood'. There are a lot of people like me, though, the underdog who went on to do OK. From Steve Jobs to Pharrell Williams, people who were considered uncool at school are the people now working in the coolest professions doing the coolest things. These are people who are unafraid to do their own thing and that's something that I really identify with.

Success does bring some difficulties, of course. I can't pop down to the supermarket for a pint of milk all that easily any more. And, the more successful you become, the more things you become committed to and it does start to feel more like 'work' rather than the thing you just used to enjoy. In some ways, I miss the control and freedom that I used to have. But the experiences I'm living through my magic make me feel so privileged. Looking back at those days hiding away in my room, sometimes I thought I'd never see anything other than those four walls and now I have the whole world at my feet. The transformation is probably the most significant magic I've ever undertaken, but it's no blink of an eye move this time. It's been a slow burner and I hope I'll carry on burning for some time to come.

♠

Although I've reached a certain stage with my magic, I never stop learning. One thing that has become a big part of my life in recent years is reading. I read as much as I can, including a lot of self-help and positive-thinking titles. Some of my favourite books include *59 Seconds: Think a Little, Change a Lot* by Professor Richard Wiseman and *One Minute Mindfulness: How to Live in the Moment* by Simon Parke. You can spend just a minute each day reading them and learn so much. With all the craziness going on around me, it's very easy to allow the pressure to overwhelm me. Some of these books put things in perspective.

I read Russell Brand's books, because he's lived a crazy life. He's one person who, from the beginning, has embraced fame. He wanted to be famous; he's done everything to get to that point. By reading books like his, they open up my mind and get me thinking creatively, which in turn helps me create new magic ideas. Because I've had a certain amount of success, it doesn't mean that I should stop pushing myself. I need to continue learning something new every day. I still have huge ambitions.

I want to change the face of magic. I want, in years to come, when someone mentions the word 'magic', for people to instantly think of 'Dynamo'. If you look at my predecessors, whenever you think of magic, the image of David Copperfield comes to mind, or in this country, Paul Daniels. But in a hundred years, when I'm long gone, I want people to think of my name like they think of Houdini. I want to leave a legacy that is that strong.

When I reflect on everything that has happened in my life so far, I do feel like I've finally arrived. I have enough confidence to say that now. I'm getting record-breaking viewing figures and winning awards left, right and centre. I was voted Britain's Coolest Man by *Zoo* magazine. Me! The school's biggest geek!

Broadcast magazine put me at number one out of the top 100 chart of TV talent. Reggie Yates was in that chart, David Beckham, and many other amazing people, and I got number one. I was even nominated at the National TV Awards, against Michael McIntyre – which he won. I didn't mind losing though – I like the guy. And, hey, you can't win 'em all!

One of the most defining moments of my magic career came in October 2011 when I was invited to join the Magic Circle, whose members include David Copperfield and Derren Brown. It's a very secretive organisation so all I can really reveal is that I'm an associate member of the Inner Magic Circle and I was given the prestigious Silver Star. It's a great honour and, best of all, something Gramps would have been proud of. We had talked about me joining the Magic Circle since I was a kid.

♠

One of the biggest things I wanted to achieve was to make my mum proud. It is probably one of the things that has spurred me on the most for all of these years. My mum gave birth to me when she was seventeen, so I think she missed out on a lot of teenage fun.

After she had me, she had to go back to school and so my grandparents looked after me a lot of the time. I think she sometimes feels bad about that, but she shouldn't. It isn't her fault. She was so young, just a kid. I know she's really proud of me, but sometimes I get the sense from her that she feels like she's not allowed to be proud.

People say to her, 'You raised a good one there.' I get the impression that sometimes she thinks, '*Oh, I can't take credit for it.*' But she can! Because she's my mum and she's always been there for me. She's always supported me, no matter what happened, and all she's ever wanted is for me to be happy. My mum never told me what to do. If I wanted to do something, she said, 'Try it.' She always believed in me, and not all parents do that. Mum would rather I take my own path. I love that and I love her to pieces.

In some ways, magic has brought me closer to my family, but in others – with my dad, for instance – it's pushed us further apart.

I didn't have a clue where my dad was for most of my life. He was in and out of jail so much and I never heard from him. Once, when I was about eighteen, I spoke to him and one of the first things he asked me was, 'Do you have any friends who want to shift some stuff for me?' I was like, 'You got me here to do a business deal rather than because you wanted to see your son for the first time in fourteen years?'

My mum recently had a visit from one of his friends to say that my dad was in hospital and in a coma. My dad's friend said the doctors thought he might only have a day or two left to live. He wondered if I might want to visit, but I didn't go to see him. I don't see him as a dad so I thought it might be strange. And as he hadn't personally requested, I chose not to go. A week later, my mum went to see my dad for peace of mind. He was out of the coma and making a great recovery. He didn't mind that I hadn't gone to see him. He understood. Of course, I'm glad he's still alive. Although I don't see him as a father, I wish him a long and happy life. I've had my manager Dan and my friends, girlfriend, family and colleagues around me who have given me so much support. And, even though Gramps isn't with me now, everything he taught me is. He lives on and is still supporting me in his own ways. His wise words are in my memory – there whenever I need them.

CHAPTER 15

DREAMS
CAN COME
TRUE

I've achieved so many of my dreams in the last few years. There are still lots I haven't – but you've always got to have a dream, right? And I often find myself in places that make me feel like I've come full circle. I see a little bit of Delph Hill wherever I go and it really hammers home why I need to carry on doing what I'm doing. But a moment that spurred me on more than anything happened when I visited Ukraine in 2005. Saying that it made me appreciate what I had is an understatement.

I may have had a tough time growing up, but it's nothing compared to the devastating poverty and violence that millions of people out there deal with on a daily basis. With a teenage mum and imprisoned dad, I may not have had your average family life, but I had love from my mum and grandparents, and I had food and a roof over my head.

Ukraine was eye-opening and gave me perhaps the first truly profound experience I've had while travelling. Ukraine has, or at least had, one of the highest rates of child poverty in the world. The poverty there has been described as chronic. It's really serious.

I was flown over to Kiev, the capital of Ukraine, by London nightclub promoter Nick House. A vodka company was putting on a bar-flairing event. Bar flairing is where bar tenders entertain people by manipulating their bar tools, like juggling cocktail shakers – they are the magicians of the drinks industry, perhaps! It was sponsored by *Playboy* magazine and Nick had recommended that I go over and perform.

We landed and went straight to the gig, whizzing past the banks of the Dnipro River, lined with people eating and drinking, and the elaborate gold-domed architecture for which the city is renowned. We rolled up to a huge warehouse where I would be performing. On the surface, everything was lovely, we received a warm welcome and there were lots of bartenders doing their best 'Tom Cruise in *Cocktail*' impression. If you looked a little closer, though, there was a real edginess to it. There were a lot of Russian women who appeared to be pretty high, stumbling around, being helped to their feet by burly security guys. It started to feel a little weird and quite disturbing.

After the gig, we decided to explore Kiev a little bit. We'd been told about a nightclub that was supposed to be really cool, and the promoters offered to take us out and show us the nightlife. We left this one club at about 3a.m. It was in a part of town that felt quite rough and ready. There weren't many people about and those that were seemed quite tense. We headed to the nearest taxi rank when all of a sudden we were surrounded by kids.

I was shocked. Not only was it run down, but also it was about three in the morning and there were kids everywhere. I don't mean teenagers, but actual children, four and five years old. We were surrounded by children barely out of nappies, trying to sell us flowers, chewing gum and cigarettes. Their faces were filthy, their clothes in tatters, their trainers full of holes. I jolted with a shock as I realised that they lived on the street. They had no homes. They had no parents.

Ukraine
gave me
a truly
profound
experience

Can you imagine your daughter, nephew or grandchild at four years old being so poor that they would be out all night in the streets, trying to sell flowers for the equivalent of ten pence? Can you imagine the dangers – physically and psychologically – connected with that? It broke my heart to see those kids out there. Dan gave one of the children £5 and the kid couldn't believe it; it was like he'd won the lottery. I did a piece of magic, making a coin appear from behind someone's ear and they all went mad. But then every kid wanted a coin and I realised that had been a thoughtless idea. We had upset a natural balance and unwittingly created anger and resentment among the kids. If we couldn't give something to everyone, we shouldn't have given anything to anyone.

We had to leave pretty quickly before we caused a riot. It bothered me for a long time, not just hours or days after, but throughout the following months and even now I find myself thinking about that moment a lot.

Just an hour before, I'd been in a vast warehouse space where people were ordering five or ten bottles of champagne at £800 a pop. It makes me angry to think of the over-indulgence there when there was so little elsewhere. I just wonder that if the right people were in charge, then the money could be distributed better. Rather than super rich and super poor living alongside each other, there should be a middle ground. Kids shouldn't live on the streets, full stop. I don't care what rules or regulations exist, kids shouldn't have to endure these conditions.

We were only there for a night really, but a shadow of the darkness in Kiev has been left with me. And I think that's a good thing. It instilled a strong sense of morality in me. Seeing the huge divide between rich and poor in Kiev made me much more aware of the slightly more subtle divide in this country. I made a pact to myself there and then that no matter how rich or famous

I became, I'd never be ungrateful or wasteful of my success. It helped me put my own childhood in perspective and made me appreciate what I have.

In some ways, I'm glad that it took me a long time to finally make it. If all this had happened when I was eighteen, nineteen years old, maybe I would have turned into an ego-filled monster. I'd like to think that would never have happened, but who knows. Getting the chance to experience the bigger, wider world has provided me with many invaluable lessons that have undoubtedly made me a better person than I might otherwise have been.

♠

The aching gap between the 'haves' and the 'have-nots' can be seen all over the world. From Kiev to Delph Hill, more often than not the gap between the two is out of proportion.

The problem with deprived areas, regardless of what part of the world they may be in, is the lack of opportunity. While Delph Hill kids might not have it as hard as kids in the Ukraine, both areas were similarly afflicted by a lack of inspiration. How often did those kids in Kiev get to see the five-star luxury fifteen minutes from their desperate lives? In one city or country, you have people existing in totally different worlds.

People in Delph Hill rarely leave the estate, let alone the city. They don't really have big ambitions to get out. Because of that, there's no one to look up to, there are no role models, so people don't feel inspired to do anything. It would have been very easy for me to be one of those people trapped on the estate, ending up in prison or on the dole.

I wouldn't change where I grew up at all. I think it has shaped who I am and made me appreciate everything I've been given so much more. If I wasn't from Delph Hill, I don't think I would have valued going to a place like Clarence House as much. It made it even more special, knowing where I had come from. Even though I came from an estate, I got treated with respect. Prince Charles didn't just have a polite conversation with me, he engaged with what I was saying. He really listened.

Growing up in Delph Hill, no one was there to listen to you. Everybody was trying to say something, but no one was actually listening. I think that's why a lot of communities break down. It's a struggle for power. Dog eat dog. You see it time and time again, that crabs-in-the-barrel mentality. A kid tries to leave the street to go to college – the gang pulls him back in. A vulnerable young girl with hopes and ambition ends up pregnant at fourteen years old. As soon as someone tries to break away, the people that are left behind become jealous and want to drag you back down. There are endemic issues in poor communities in the UK and around the world that need to be addressed.

A lot of people in a position of power went to grammar, boarding or public schools. Having been to a comprehensive, I can testify how difficult it is to achieve much when the school has a low pass average, poor attendance rates and high levels of anti-social behaviour. It feels like kids at your average comprehensive aren't expected to do more than pass and leave – maybe you'll go to college, maybe you won't. If you do have aspirations to attend university, can you or your mum (and dad if you're lucky enough to have both in your life) afford the rising fees? Maybe, if you're in the top ten per cent of the exceptionally bright, you might win a scholarship. How about the kid whose intelligence is just above average? What happens to him?

I'm not saying that some jobs are better than others and everyone should strive to be a lawyer over a hairdresser – my mum is a brilliant hairdresser! I just wish there was more choice for young people to allow them to pursue something they are passionate about – whatever that might be. They should be able to have the option of being a lawyer OR a hairdresser, whichever they care more about.

That's why I admire people like Richard Branson, Oprah Winfrey and Will Smith. They came from nothing, they were normal working-class kids and they've each built their own businesses and have focused on a career that truly motivated them. These men and women have had rejection after rejection, failure after failure, but they refused to give up.

It makes me feel like it doesn't matter how many new magic ideas I come up with, I won't be able to rest until I've made one special transformation happen. I want my magic to help others make their dreams come true even if it's just in a small way.

I hope that what I do can inspire other people. I hope that I can show people that you can make something from nothing, whatever that might be. With hard work, determination and a little bit of good luck, you can defy the odds. You can break the cycle. I always say that luck is when preparation and hard work meets opportunity. I have been preparing for this moment for over fifteen years and at times I didn't know if it was ever going to happen, but I kept on going. I'm not meant to be able to walk on water or fly through the air, but I do. I'd urge anyone else to truly believe they can do whatever they want to. Nothing is impossible.

If me – a kid from Bradford with no proper education – can do it, anyone can. When I was growing up, I didn't really have people to look to for inspiration apart from the make-believe superheroes in films and Gramps, of course. But if somebody notices me, somebody real, who has broken out from the estate and succeeded, and I inspire that person (even if it's just the one), then I will know in my heart that magic really does exist...

EPILOGUE

KEEPING THE MAGIC ALIVE

've saved this moment of my life until last because it is the single most real thing I have ever had to deal with. It stands apart from anything else and has changed my life forever. When Gramps, Kenneth Walsh, died aged eighty-four, magic became the only thing in life that I knew I could depend on. The one thing that would never leave me.

If it wasn't for Gramps, I don't know how life would have turned out. My great-grandfather was always there for me. He not only introduced me to magic, he was also the man who taught me to swim, who showed me how to ride my first bike, who did my homework with me. I remember he used to drive around the estate in his white Vauxhall Astra. I thought it was the coolest car ever, mostly because he was the only person I knew who had a car! He used to pick me up and take me to football, or we'd go fishing. He was the coolest guy ever. He might have been my great-grandfather, but he had a lot of energy for a man of his age. He was magical in every sense of the word. It was only in the last few years of his life that he was stuck in a wheelchair. Before then, he had more energy and spark than me and my friends put together. He embraced life and all he had to give.

Having served in the Second World War, Gramps used magic as a way of entertaining the other soldiers and keeping their spirits up. He always cast a light on the darkest of situations. After the war, he returned home to a severe economic depression. But he managed to get a job working in the mills which was proper, physical, hard work. He made little money and was only able to put little bits of food on the table, but he always got by. Gramps wasn't a magician really; he only used magic to win a beer. Small things when rations were tight in Bradford. Magic made him a little bit of money here and there. Well, apart from on one occasion, when he managed to bag himself a woman! My nan, the ultimate prize! My nan, Nelly, had met Gramps not long after she had given birth to my grandma, Nana Lynne. She had broken up with my birth great-granddad, and she and Ken were together from then on in. He was very close to my mum and, through her, close to me. So he was in fact my step-great-granddad, but that is an inconsequential fact as far as I'm concerned. He was a real granddad to me.

Gramps was also a proper man's man. He was strong but he had humility. And he protected his own. He loved Nan to pieces. It's very rare that you see couples that have been together for so long. Whenever I saw them it was so obvious how in love they were. You don't see that much in this day and age.

Gramps saved me from the bullies when I was twelve years old, he inspired my love of magic and he taught me everything I needed to know as a magician. Even as I got older, Gramps was always there for me. I didn't speak to him on the phone as much, because he had trouble hearing as he got older, so I made sure I visited him every week. It wasn't always easy when I moved to London, so every moment I did get at home was precious. When I was around Gramps, I wouldn't want to talk about anything negative. I wouldn't want to bring it into that warm environment.

He had this weird way about him, and so always kept things positive when I was in his company. In a way I forgot my troubles when I was with him. True magic. By the time I left his house, I would be feeling inspired. Nothing would faze me.

I think he knew how much he meant to me. Although we wouldn't have those kinds of conversations when we were together, I know he read the interviews and saw the television programmes where I always bigged him up. I think the time it really hit home for him was when I turned up with a tattoo of his nickname 'Gramps' on my neck. That year he'd had a couple of strokes and when he saw the tattoo it was the first time I had seen him smile all year. I put it there so I would always know that he was there looking over my shoulder, keeping an eye on my magic. He was in hospital when I showed him my tattoo. He smiled warmly and then drifted off to sleep.

It was a proud smile.

Gramps was like a father and a grandfather to me. When he died on 29 February 2012, I took the news very hard. He had been ill for a while, but had taken a bad turn overnight. He had had three strokes and was suffering from a brain tumour. Gramps was told he only had days to live. When he died, I rushed home to Bradford for a few weeks. I just needed to be at home. I was filming the second series of *Dynamo: Magician Impossible* at that point, but I had to send the cameras away. I didn't really want to be filmed. I didn't want to talk to anyone or see anyone. It was like the magic had died with him. I had no drive, no ambition. I felt numb.

The night Gramps died, I was in Bradford. I'd driven up there with my girlfriend to visit him. We dropped off our stuff at a hotel and then went to see him in the hospice. He was very ill at that point and in a deep sleep, so we weren't sure if he knew we were there. Me, my nan, who was there with him all the time, and my girlfriend sat in the hospice and chatted to him and each other. We watched an episode of *My Big Fat Gypsy Wedding* because my nan loves it.

Later that night, we left the hospice and drove to the hotel. We'd been asleep for about two hours when the hotel phone started ringing. It was 1.40am and I immediately got a strange feeling in my stomach. I hesitated to pick up the phone, scared of what I might hear.

It was the nurse from the hospice ringing to tell me that Gramps had just passed away. Stunned, I put the phone back on its cradle, turned to my girlfriend and started to cry. I cried myself to sleep in her arms.

I slept very, very deeply. I woke up the next day and actually felt OK, which was weird in itself. I think I was probably still in shock. Even though I knew how ill Gramps was, I just couldn't believe he'd actually gone. I couldn't believe I'd never see him again.

I went to Starbucks to get some coffees and it was there that it hit me. All of a sudden, I was surrounded by people, asking for autographs and pictures. There were people everywhere and all I could think was 'He's gone, Gramps is gone.' I had to pretend to be OK, and so I kept on smiling and taking pictures. But it took everything in my power not to drop the coffees and run out. I just wanted to be by myself.

That first night was the only time I cried over Gramps. I didn't cry at the funeral. I can't explain why. But I guess I knew that Gramps wouldn't want to me to be upset. I didn't want to go to the funeral because I don't think funerals are the best way to remember someone. But that's only my opinion. I went to Gramps' service for Nan and Mum, though, to support them. They asked me to give a speech.

As with everything I do, I improvised. I said something along the lines of, 'Everyone knows my grandpa. He was like a father figure to me. He raised me, got me into magic, he is the reason I do what I do today. I know it's a sad day, but Gramps wouldn't want us to be down. He'd want us to have a good time and get down to the pub and celebrate his life, so let's do it.'

It took some time, but eventually, I began to do magic again. Once I started it became my way of coping with the loss. It was another example of the power magic has. Whenever life is hard, magic continues to rescue me.

Gramps was the main male role model in my life, the person who I looked up to. He also never discouraged me from doing anything I wanted. Anything. He filled me with confidence.

Before he was ill I think I only ever saw him unhappy twice in my whole life; he was always happy. Even when he was sick, he would make a joke out of anything. No matter how I was feeling, or, indeed, how he was feeling, he would always cheer me up. He was my salvation as a kid. He inspired me in every way. He was a great man. He was my superstar.

Gramps introduced me to magic and magic changed my life. It took me to places I never dreamed I'd visit, showed me the most amazing sights and introduced me to so many extraordinary people. It opened doors for me and continues to do so today. And when I was in a dark place when Gramps died, it was magic that gradually drew me into the sunlight again.

Gramps, I love you and always will. Thank you for showing me there is magic in the world. Now that I've found it, I'll keep hold of it, always, and make sure that our magic lives on.

To everyone who has believed in this impossible dream of mine. I couldn't have done it without you.

ABOUT THE AUTHOR

Dynamo was born Steven Frayne in December 1982 in Bradford.
He grew up on the notorious Delph Hill housing estate, where he
was raised by his mother while his father spent long periods in
prison. At the same time, he was forced to battle a debilitating
form of Crohn's disease as well as deal with playground bullies.

After being introduced to magic by his beloved granddad,
and receiving a loan from The Prince's Trust, he carved out a
career as one of the world's most respected magicians and
illusionists. His TV series *Dynamo: Magician Impossible* has broken
all viewing records for UKTV channel Watch and has won three
Broadcast Awards.

Dynamo now lives in London where he continues to dream up
even bigger and better illusions to prove to the world that really
nothing is impossible. This is his first book.

PICTURE CREDITS

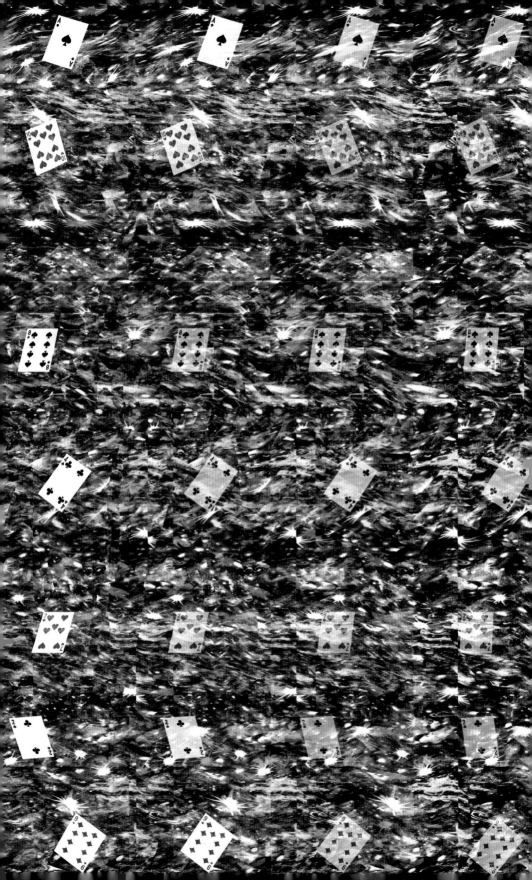